UNIVERSITY TRENDS

CONTEMPORARY CAMPUS DESIGN

JONATHAN COULSON
PAUL ROBERTS
ISABELLE TAYLOR

 Routledge
Taylor & Francis Group

LONDON AND NEW YORK

First published 2015
by Routledge
2 Park Square, Milton Park, Abingdon, Oxon OX14 4RN

and by Routledge
711 Third Avenue, New York, NY 10017

Routledge is an imprint of the Taylor & Francis Group, an informa business

British Library Cataloguing-in-Publication Data
A catalogue record for this book is available from the British Library

Library of Congress Cataloging-in-Publication Data
Coulson, Jonathan, author.
University trends : contemporary campus design / Jonathan Coulson,
Paul Roberts and Isabelle Taylor.
pages cm
Includes bibliographical references and index.
1. College buildings. 2. Campus planning. I. Roberts, Paul (Michael Paul),
1964- author. II. Taylor, Isabelle, author. III. Title.

ISBN: 978-1-138-79729-1 (hbk)
ISBN: 978-1-135-75720-9 (ebk)

Printed in Great Britain by Bell & Bain Ltd, Glasgow

MIX
Paper from
responsible sources
FSC® C007785
FSC www.fsc.org

Cover: The Hub, Coventry University (2011)

Page 4: Swanston Academic Building, RMIT (2012)

ACKNOWLEDGMENTS

A large number of people have contributed to and assisted in the realization of this book. To all those who gave their time and help we extend our thanks. Acknowledgements go to Dave Gibson of Draught Associates for designing the book. In particular, we would like to recognize the contributions of several of our colleagues at Turnberry: Josh Martin, Chris Pattison, Frances Richie, Bethania Soriano, and Victoria Webster.

CONTENTS

PREFACE

The campus has a deep-rooted prestige as a place of teaching, learning, and nurturing. Conjuring images of cloistered quadrangles, of sunny lawns, of wood-panelled libraries cloaked in an ethereal hush, it is a word viscerally charged with centuries of scholarly tradition. And yet it is also a place of cutting-edge science, of youth, vibrancy, and energy. It is this dual nature, this concurrent adherence to tradition and innovation, which renders the physical environment of the university such a redolent, enduring, and dynamic realm. However, it also means that the twenty-first-century campus is a highly challenging and exacting landscape to design and manage successfully. A city in miniature, it must continually respond to external political and fiscal pressures, whilst simultaneously adapting to changing pedagogies and technology.

We have been involved in the strategic planning and design of universities for a number of years, working with institutions across the higher education spectrum, from the centuries-old to the brand-new, from the most urban settings to greenfield sites. What is becoming progressively more palpable – and what motivated the research that has evolved into this book – is that answering the administrative, pedagogic, and financial demands of a higher education institution is more exacting than ever. It is a critical moment for higher education: squeezed public spending, rising tuition fees, and the growing education ambitions of developing nations, are set against a backdrop of rapid technological progress. The experience of writing a survey book about the global history of campus planning and architecture (*University Planning and Architecture: The Search for Perfection*, 2010) heightened our awareness of the rich, fluid trajectory of this discipline, and the formative influence that the physical environment can wield in shaping and reflecting institutional ideologies and identities. What of the future though? What impact is the current context having upon this evolution and this influence? How is it impacting upon the physical environment of the university, as qualified by the term campus? These are the questions that are contemplated here.

University Trends sets out to broadly take stock of the contemporary climate of the discipline of university master planning and architecture. This field is undergoing a continuous evolution to answer to the kinetic financial, pedagogic, strategic, and technological climate of higher education. From a national and international perspective, we examine how this is happening by reviewing contemporary master planning and building projects. Its objective is to identify and outline the most widespread, consequential, and dynamic design 'trends' that are shaping the planning and architecture of higher education institutions across the world today, and those that look set to do so in the future.

The book is divided into two sections. Part I establishes what we consider these trends to be, organized first into single-building typologies and followed by master planning practices:

- — Adaptive reuse
- — Starchitecture
- — Hub buildings
- — Interdisciplinary science research buildings
- — Joint-venture buildings
- — New universities beyond the West
- — Transnational education
- — Commercial urban developments
- — Large-scale campus expansions
- — Revitalizing master plans
- — Online learning

The list inevitably simplifies the complex and fecund developments within campus design by condensing them into only 11 categories. We are not aspiring to an exhaustive inventory of the building and planning archetypes featuring within capital project schedules, neither is it a review of pedagogic or market strategies within higher education. Our rationale has been to identify the most prominent, thought provoking, or loaded building and master-planning typologies that are determining the physical environments in which tertiary learning is taking place. The list of trends excludes as specific categories, for example, student residences, which have long been a vital component of the campus. Although these are being built in rising numbers globally to accommodate growing student populations, they were not included here as the approach to their design and planning has not undergone any marked transformations. Likewise, the list does not include sustainability. This is a criterion which is fundamental to almost every design and construction project at almost every university across the globe. Whole books have been devoted to this theme, and thus rather than demarcate it as a specific trend we are interpreting the application of sustainability principles as an unwritten canon.

After each theme is reviewed, Part I will move from the present to the future. The section will end with a forecast of the priorities of campus design in forthcoming years. Which of these trends will survive, how will they evolve, and what will be the prime concerns of those charged with shaping the built environment of higher education? We give a conjectural assessment.

In Part II, the trends are encapsulated in a series of case studies profiling individual buildings and master planning projects, which represent superlative examples or instructional aspects of each category. (The exception is online learning, whose nature means that it has not given rise to physical projects.) To ensure the relevance of these schemes they are all drawn from the three-year period 2011–13, being either completed, designed, or, in the case of long-running master planning endeavours, having reached a significant juncture during this timespan. Out of the countless master planning and building ventures recently or currently being undertaken by universities across the world, we only have the scope here to feature but a small proportion. Many worthy or interesting schemes are not featured, but in those that did survive the final cut we have attempted to embrace a comprehensive range in terms of their geography and scale, encompassing both the high-profile and the less-familiar.

It is important to note that the classifications of trends are not hard and fast, but fluid and flexible. The same projects may overlap one, two, or more of the trends. For instance, Monash University's New Horizons Centre (2013) in Melbourne, a research complex housing scientists from the university and Australia's national government-funded R&D body, can be bracketed within both the Interdisciplinary Buildings and the Joint-Venture Buildings groups. Likewise, North West Cambridge – a £1-billion greenfield development by the University of Cambridge comprising academic and research facilities, student accommodation, market housing, retail, and community amenities – qualifies for inclusion within the categories of large-scale expansion and commercial urban design projects. This fluidity itself speaks of the increasingly integrated, protean, and interdisciplinary nature of higher education.

We will close this preamble where we began – with a reassertion of the value of the campus as a physical place. These variegated institutions are growing more complex with every academic year that passes, engendering a new repertoire of building typologies and planning priorities. Through its analysis of current schemes and its meditation on the future, *University Trends* aspires to decoct this fluctuating and complicated, but rewarding field.

Jonathan Coulson and Paul Roberts
February 2014

ONE

THE TWENTY-FIRST CENTURY CAMPUS

THE CONTEXT

Since the founding of the modern world's first universities 900 years ago, institutions of higher education have given rise to some of the world's most emotive, hallowed, and formative physical environments. The idea of a university education is inviolably associated with the idea of place. The steps of the library, the arcades of the faculty building, the lawns where lazy afternoons are spent, these are the backdrop against which the experience of academic life in all its complexity occurs. A university's physical setting must meet the operational demands placed upon it, but its remit extends far beyond function. Buildings and landscapes lie at the heart and soul of the university community.

Academic reputation is undoubtedly the foremost objective of any higher education institution. However, this alone does not suffice. Pioneering architecture and coherent campus planning make for vivid assertions of institutional identity, reinforcing scholastic ideals and values, which can dually boost its image and act as a focus for community spirit. Moreover, all but the most exclusive universities are facing increasing competition for students and staff, and the appearance of a campus can play a critical role in tipping the balance. Although somewhat crude, this is a realistic assessment.

The augmentation of the higher education industry and its fierce competition for the best students has bred a growing receptiveness amongst higher education institutions (HEIs) to the importance of their environment. While not confined to the twenty-first century, this mind-set has sharply intensified since the turn of the century. The net result has been significant investment in physical infrastructure, especially in the US. 'If you build it, they will come' is how the *New York Times* in 2012 described the approach pursued by American college administrators. The building boom at North American universities has been ardent. Construction starts there rose from 1.12 million square metres (12.1 million square feet) in 1990 to 3 million square metres (32.6 million square feet) in 2008.[1] Major and minor universities alike set in motion large-scale expansion plans, such as the scheme issued by the University of Pennsylvania in Philadelphia in 2006 which called for infill expansion on the main campus plus the redevelopment of 10 hectares (24 acres) hitherto owned by the U.S. Postal Service; or the 7-hectare (17-acre), Renzo Piano-designed campus expansion announced by Columbia University in 2003,

its first major expansion in 75 years. To a less zealous extent, UK universities also entered into a building race, followed more recently by Australian counterparts. The University of Leicester in the UK, for instance, unveiled a £300 million scheme in 2002 to expand building space by 30 per cent; in Melbourne, Monash University launched a campus vision in 2011 which will see the floor area of its Caulfield campus grow by 87 per cent to some 168,000 square metres (1.8 million square feet).

As higher education grows, it is becoming increasingly difficult to perpetuate the rich tradition of campus design. With each passing year, universities are challenged by an evolving repertoire of external forces creating long-term and immediate pressures which the built environment must respond to and support. Not least of these is the recent worldwide economic crisis. The tangible impact this has had upon the physical landscape of higher education is hard to overestimate.

The financial collapse of 2008 created an unprecedented and harrowing climate for university administrators. America's campus building surge came to an almost blanket halt; globally few tertiary education institutions went unscathed by the collapse of the economic markets. At Harvard University, the world's richest, the second half of 2008 saw its endowment shrink from $36.9 billion to $28.8 billion.[2] The derailment of Harvard's ambitious new development in Allston, across the river from its historic Cambridge campus, was highly publicized. In 2009, it was forced to stop construction of a $1.4 billion science centre by Behnisch Architekten, notwithstanding its foundations had already been completed.[3] The same year, Princeton University postponed $695 million worth of construction projects. Much smaller projects, such as an £850,000 extension at the University of Newcastle, have also been subject to indefinite delays. In the UK, government funding allocated to capital works plummeted from £455 million in 2010/11 to £182 million in 2013.[4]

The so-called 'Edifice Complex' left many institutions burdened with debt after the financial crisis hit. Amidst extensive expansion works, New York University for example saw its debt more than double in less than a decade from $1.2 billion in 2002 to $2.8 billion in 2011.[5] Harvard's annual financial report for 2012 painted an unusually sobering portrait of the current climate: 'The need for change in higher education is clear given the emerging disconnect between ever-increasing aspirations and universities' ability to generate the new resources to finance them.'[6]

The sting of falling investment values, private donations, and state funding is a biting reality for universities. Yet this situation must be managed in tandem with the concurrent demands to accommodate growing numbers of students. The UK, for example, saw a rapid surge in total numbers from just under two million in 2000/1 to around 2.5 million in 2010/11, in part due to a boom in international students coming primarily from Asia.[7] Moreover, with competition for the best applicants more intense than ever, students are expecting more from their facilities. The mantra of the student as customer is firmly entrenched. British universities are attempting to expiate the recent jump in tuition fees with new buildings; a 2013 survey revealed that nearly 80 per cent of the nation's higher education bodies intended to spend more than £5 million on construction projects in the following year to attract students.[8] Forced into competition not only amongst themselves but now increasingly with their compeers on the other side of the Atlantic and mainland Europe, British universities have replaced shared showers and draughty libraries with ensuites and free Wi-Fi to satisfy the ever-higher expectations of the student population. The matter becomes more critical when one considers the need to attract high-paying international students. It is a case of keeping up with the Joneses on a worldwide scale.

The higher education marketplace is progressively widening beyond its traditional Anglo preserve. Western campuses have benefited substantially from the appetite for places from students of emerging countries, who typically encounter higher tuition fees than home applicants. But this pattern may be evolving. Higher education is internationalizing in leaps and bounds. Predictions are plentiful for the global rise in total student numbers, and while the figures themselves do not always correspond, there is unanimous consensus that this figure will soar fuelled by the ambitions of developing and undeveloped economies to foster knowledge economies.[9]

Traditional feeder countries, such as Malaysia, Singapore, and China, are striving to become education destinations themselves by amplifying the range and quality of their higher education provision. China, for instance, is assertively seeking to boost its international profile. In 2009 it formalized its C9 League, a group of nine institutions pitched as the country's 'Ivy League' and targeted for extra funding to further world-class excellence. Together they receive about 10 per cent of China's R & D expenditures.[10] The country aims to boost its enrollment of foreign students by 2020 to 500,000, up from 2013 levels of 260,000.[11] Hong Kong, meanwhile, in a desire to become an 'education hub' for the region, has raised quotas on the number of non-domestic students from 10 per cent to 20 per cent of the total enrollment.[12] Non-Anglo universities are likely to emerge as important actors within the commodification of transnational

education. In what may prove to be a harbinger of future patterns, Zhejiang University, a member of the C9, opened talks in 2013 with Imperial College London to occupy part of its new campus in west London.[13]

It is not only the loci of higher education that are shifting, moreover. Institutions are tackling radical changes in the methods of teaching and research, fuelled by the soaring pace of technology. Technological developments are blurring the boundaries of the traditional built learning environment. The didactic lecture-theatre model is waning. Fewer and fewer conventional, stand-alone lecture theatres are being commissioned, as learning becomes ever more a collaborative process engaging a growing repertoire of informal spaces on and off campus. The technology infrastructure of the nineteenth- and twentieth-century campus cannot keep step with the twenty-first-century learning climate, necessitating changes in approach to the physical environment. Libraries are an obvious subject of this evolution. Their single-purpose remit to foster private study amongst shelf after shelf of books is expanding to include computer-based research, group study, interactive instruction and often cafés, as reflected in the changing nomenclature from 'library' to 'learning commons' or 'learning resource centre'. 'What was once a simple ordered world of books and journals has become a complex and plural place,' author Brian Edwards has noted.[14] Its building typology – for generations, static in its basic form – is changing to reflect this.

In the transition from nineteenth-century traditions to a twenty-first-century 'immersive learningscape', the need for agile, flexible spaces that are capable of responding to future advances is becoming progressively more important. Increasingly, the conventional commissioning process is evolving away from the rigorous specifications of discrete facilities or disciplines towards more generalized calls for community interaction and multi-layered spaces. This is relevant not only for individual buildings but also when considering the wider urban realm of the campus.

Universities large and small are reacting to this changing climate. The shifts in learning practices, in the global education market, in student expectations, and in financial outlook are having marked ramifications for the university estate. This is resulting in an evolving lexicon of building and master plan types or, as we have dubbed them, 'trends'. The following section will sketch the most influential, salient, and pervasive of the trends in architecture typologies and master planning that are currently at work at HEIs around the world, beginning with the time-honoured practice of repurposing a structure for a function its builders never imagined.

ADAPTIVE REUSE

The old wives' adage 'waste not, want not' has gained revived currency in recent years. The prolonged financial crisis has tightened many belts, engendering a 'make do and mend' spirit across nearly all walks of life. It is an attitude which has made sizeable inroads into the architectural world. Tearing down existing buildings to replace them with dazzling new versions has fast lost popularity in some markets in favour of adaptive reuse, the name given to the practice whereby old buildings are converted to something better suited to modern needs.

The repurposing of a building for an activity other than its original function is often engaged to protect historically or architecturally significant structures from abandonment, deterioration, and demolition. It is far from a modern phenomenon. Pagan temples were transformed into Christian churches, and English monasteries became country estates. Converting existing buildings is a matter of common-sense economics which has taken place throughout history, including at universities. The dissolved nunnery of St Radegund in Cambridge, UK, was repurposed as Jesus College in the 1590s; Bangor University in Wales opened its doors in October 1884 in an old coaching inn; in the US, in 1946 Roosevelt University moved into a nineteenth-century theatre, hotel, and office building in Chicago designed by Louis Sullivan; whilst the University of Alcalá in Spain adapted a military aerodrome in the late 1960s.

Reuse has been vaulted to prominence within architectural theory and practice once again. The financial strictures of recent years have encouraged a more widespread and creative attitude to retrofitting and repurposing. Meanwhile, several high-profile efforts by superstar-level practitioners, including David Chipperfield's restoration of the Neues Museum in Berlin (2009), Diller Scofidio + Renfro's renewal of New York's High Line (2009, 2011), and Rem Koolhaas's 2010 appointment to modernize the St Petersburg Hermitage, have leant a fashionable kudos to preservation.[15]

The decision to adopt an adaptive reuse methodology can be laden with ethical and practical considerations. Many architecturally-important buildings are awarded historic status, often entailing rigid conditions which prevent structural modifications. Successful reuse necessitates not only a sensitive response to the integrity of the building, but also rigorous study of its existing architectural fabric. The constraints that this fabric may embody are of critical importance when it comes to accommodating new functions. In other words, a fundamental question to ask of any adaptive reuse candidate, is whether the building's form can feasibly be reshaped to suit its proposed new role. Adaptive reuse is simply not viable in all instances.

Nevertheless, despite the challenges and debate that adaptive reuse occasions, it offers great possibilities. Conversion schemes are amongst some of the most imaginative and intelligent projects that the architecture world can boast, particularly in their scope for environmental responsibility. Razing and rebuilding existing building stock ranks amongst the most profligate expenditure of natural resources. New construction accounts for 40 per cent of the total flow of raw materials globally.[16] Enormous quantities of energy are consumed in raw material extraction, processing, transportation, and construction, not to mention the ecological cost associated with demolition in terms of landfill, to the extent that it takes an estimated 65 years for an energy-efficient new building to recapture the amount of energy lost in demolishing an existing one.[17] At a time of increasing environmental awareness, reuse can provide an efficient means of meeting new spatial requirements at a mitigated environmental cost.

Financial costs, too, may also be tempered. The unexpected challenges that repurposing an historical buildings can raise means that reuse is frequently not a cheap option. Nonetheless it is typically less expensive than new construction, a factor that even the most dedicated patrons of contemporary construction are increasingly receptive to, particularly institutions of higher education.

In a climate where development opportunities both greenfield and brownfield attract acute public scrutiny, adaptive reuse has been adopted by universities as an

astute means of providing for higher education's growing and changing spatial requirements. Great ingenuity has been displayed in the conversion of a surprising range of existing buildings, never intended for academic use. In 2008, the Vrije Universiteit Brussel in Belgium repurposed a two-level car park as the Department of Architecture, whilst four years later at the Eindhoven University of Technology in the Netherlands, a 1959 boilerhouse was converted into laboratory and office space.

Mid-twentieth-century campuses, like Eindhoven and Vrije Universiteit Brussel, frequently find themselves requiring alteration at a faster pace than their predecessors. The postwar years brought a spirit of optimism and innovation that led many campuses to embrace ambitious modern design, not withstanding the shortages of finance and materials that followed World War II. Deliberately striving to break links with the past, architects were driven by the maxim of functionality. However, today many buildings of this generation are undermined by the poor quality of their materials and construction, and by their specificity of function. Highly specific structures such as Boston University's Law

Tower (1964) in the US set themselves up for obsolescence soon after their completion. The tower lacks the classrooms, seminar space, and common social amenities considered requisite for twenty-first-century academic buildings, and thus is currently preparing for a full rehabilitation and addition to enable it to support modern teaching methods and practices.

Construction from the second half of the twentieth century can lend itself to change more readily than its forerunners. Non-load-bearing walls, open-plan layouts, and grid plans facilitate this. Yet these structures often require cosmetic change due to their unpopularity on campus. In Britain, for instance, the University of Birmingham created a new home for its School of Sport and Exercise Science in 2005 by part-use of a 1965 engineering block. The project stripped the building back to its skeleton, adding a new façade of aluminium and timber.

It is not only campus buildings of certain eras, but also buildings of certain types that require more frequent adaptation than others. Science buildings in particular have been vulnerable to the swift pace of technological progress in the twentieth century. In 2011 at a cost of $42 million, Brown University in the US reconfigured its Metcalf Laboratories, built in the 1920s for chemistry teaching and research, for use by the Department of Cognitive, Linguistic and Psychological Services. The university had originally planned for a completely new building until the economic downturn turned adaptive reuse into a much more attractive proposition.[18] Brown has a lengthy record of similar projects, not only reusing its own building stock but existing city structures also. Since its founding in 1770, the college has grown to include over 235 buildings, 75 per cent of which were built before 1955 and a mere 18 per cent of these were built by Brown itself.

As the case of Brown illustrates, universities are not only finding opportunities for adaptive reuse within their own estate but amongst structures never intended for academic uses. Brown's campus, for example, includes over 100 houses. Similarly, in Manhattan, New York University has expanded into a variety of properties surrounding its Greenwich Village core that were originally intended for domestic use. This practice not only answers necessity, but can also be of value in building or enhancing campus identity and town–gown interaction, particularly for urban institutions. As a generalization, old buildings have a place rooted in the community, whether this be as a place of work, worship, culture, or leisure, that a modern replacement simply is not immediately entitled to. Historical buildings play an important role in the formation, accumulation, and dissemination of the collective memory of place; superlative historic or architectural credentials are not necessarily requisite for this. For a university, the sensitive adaptive

reuse of such a structure can bolster community relations, as local residents unite through a passion for a well-loved building, whether this be an architectural icon, a place of historic importance, or the site of shared memory.

Amongst the most illustrative cases of this attitude is the Savannah College of Art and Design (SCAD). Founded in 1978 in the Georgia port city of Savannah, SCAD has followed a model of adaptive reuse for over 30 years to meet the needs of its growing campus. It purchased its first, and now flagship, premises, the Volunteer Guards Armory (1892) in 1978 which, despite being one of Savannah's first examples of Romanesque Revival, was essentially abandoned at the time. Since then, the college has purchased and converted nearly 280,000 square metres (three million square feet) of building space spanning the entire period of the city's lifetime from the antebellum era to the present, much of which would almost certainly otherwise have been lost to the wrecker's ball. It has repurposed a vast range of building types: its student centre, for example, is a former synagogue; an abandoned department store became its library; and the university museum occupies a complex once owned by the Central of Georgia Railway. This approach to campus development is not only environmentally commendable and budget friendly, but has enabled the college, which is still relatively young, to integrate and take root within its host city. 'Putting the school in restored treasures helped establish SCAD more than anything,' confirmed founder Richard Rowan. 'No one thinks of us as a new college. People pass by our buildings every day and think we've been here for 100 years.'[19] Adaptive reuse has become the key element of SCAD's brand.

The college has not confined this model to Savannah. As it has expanded to Atlanta, Lacoste in France, and most recently Hong Kong, its campuses have followed the precedent of adaptive reuse of both historic and non-historic structures. SCAD acquired its 31-building estate in France in 2002 from the painter Bernard Pfriem, who had built up a collection of abandoned buildings and renovated them into artist residences. The former

Opposite above: SCAD's French outpost is housed within a small medieval village in Provence, with school buildings dating to the 12th, 15th and 16th centuries.

Opposite below: In 2010 SCAD opened a Hong Kong campus based in a 1960s courthouse.

Designed by GMP architects, the main building of Hamburg-Harburg Technical University comprises contemporary glass, steel, and aluminium extensions added to the listed structures of a World War II barracks.

village bakery is now SCAD Lacoste's library. The Hong Kong campus opened in 2010 at a former judicial centre, the North Kowloon Magistery (1960). One of its courtrooms was kept intact, to become a lecture room; jail cells became offices and conference rooms; the staff canteen is now an art gallery; while the car park was remodelled into a library.

Higher education has embraced adaptive reuse on a variety of scales and using a range of typologies; indeed the breadth of this over recent years is prodigious. From modest-sized projects, like the University of Queensland's redevelopment of a 1913 boilerhouse into a 418-square-metre (4,500-square-foot) Community Engagement Centre (2006), adaptive reuse can soar up the scale to whole campuses, such as the Saint-Charles University in Montpellier, France. Here, a seventeenth-century hospital is being given new life as an education campus in a dramatic, phased scheme (first stage completed 2011). Furthermore, whilst some adaptive reuse projects are realized wholly within the boundaries of an existing building envelope, such as SCAD Hong Kong, others combine old with new construction, such as Central Saint Martins Granary Building (UK, see pages 68–71), Harvard's New College Theatre (now Farkas Hall, 2007), and the Hamburg-Harburg Technical University in Germany, based at the former Schwarzenberg Barracks. The latter created a main building in 2012 by extending the shell of an existing red-brick military building with two flanking cubes. Although matching the original building in height and scale, the new additions embraced a modern vocabulary of glass, aluminium tubes, and stainless steel cables.

Such projects are far from simple and may not carry the headline-generating allure of new construction. However, by reclaiming land and buildings that have become obsolete or unloved, universities have the potential to leave heritage legacies, inviting innovative architectural solutions that can build an institution's brand, nurture community relations, and be environmentally responsible.

STARCHITECTURE

Daniel Libeskind's characteristically-crystalline Run Run Shaw Creative Media Centre opened in 2011 at the City University of Hong Kong.

Most people with an interest in architecture are familiar with the architectural fairytale of Bilbao, the down-at-heel industrial town on the northern Spanish coast that was propelled to international fame and fortune overnight with the opening of Frank Gehry's jaw-dropping Guggenheim Museum in 1997. The building mesmerized audiences, transforming the economically-distressed city into a global travel destination. Thanks to the power of mass media, the structure became a celebrity in itself. The impact of this single world-class project on the fortunes of the faded Basque city has come to be termed the 'Bilbao effect'.

The lure of the Bilbao effect proved irresistible. Other cities across the world immediately sat up and took notice; department stores, company headquarters, and university campuses grasped the captivating potential of a landmark public building. 'A spectre is haunting the global village – the spectre of the iconic building,' wrote leading theorist Charles Jencks in his 2005 survey of this recent architectural episode. 'Driven by social forces, the demand for instant fame and economic growth, the expressive landmark has challenged

the previous tradition of the architectural monument.'[20] Avant-garde iconic architecture powered by a breed of media-friendly architects was heralded as a near-certain route to successful branding. The phenomenon even generated its own sobriquets: 'starchitecture' and 'starchitects'.

The monikers are frequently repudiated by architecture professionals and critics, but they have nevertheless endured. In an age which is saturated by the 'cult of celebrity', the labels embody the concept of celebrity as manifested in the context of architecture. A small and exclusive club, 'starchitects' bring recognition and value to a project through their name alone, delivering buildings which are as 'recognizable as a corporate logo or an Armani suit'.[21] Gehry's colliding, fluid metal forms or Daniel Libeskind's angular contours have, thanks to media attention, become signature styles readily recalled in the public imagination.

Often derided as causes célèbres and prima donnas, 'starchitect' buildings have nonetheless succeeded in pushing contemporary architecture into the minds of the wider public. This is especially true in consideration of the campus. Celebrity architects and eye-catching design are no new thing in the realm of the university. In the UK, Christopher Wren's Sheldonian Theatre at Oxford or in the US, Thomas Jefferson's Lawn at the University of Virginia, and Eero Saarinen's Kresge Auditorium at the Massachusetts Institute of Technology (MIT) have all become icons, yet they were not originally conceived to be vehicles of this headline-carrying status. Over the past two decades, however, the 'spectre of the iconic building' has assumed a salient place in the estate strategies of university administrators. MIT has been a torchbearer of this trend, inaugurating a billion-dollar building programme in the 1990s to transform drab, neglected areas of its campus into architectural showpieces. It enlisted luminaries of the profession including Steven Holl, whose dormitory Simmons Hall opened in 2002, and Gehry, who designed the Stata Centre laboratory complex which opened two years later. From the moment their designs were revealed, these structures became instant talking points, and they continue to be such.

As one writer has phrased it, a 'starchitect' building can create 'an aura of anticipation of what will happen in that "place"'.[22] This capacity to spark attention has become a valuable marketing tool to university administrators within an increasingly competitive and crowded higher education field. It is no coincidence that starchitecture structures often occupy prominent, gateway positions on campus, such as the forthcoming arts complex by Santiago Calatrava at Yuan Ze University in Taiwan. High-profile architects can attract donors, can brand the institution as cutting edge, and for young or less-renowned universities can serve to place them on the map and boost enrollments. For example, as part of an attempt to reinvent itself from technical college into an elite institution, Lüneburg University in Germany has not only changed its name to Leuphana but in 2009 commissioned Libeskind to design a new main building. Libeskind's signature aesthetic of acute angles and crystalline forms are held by the school's officials as a sure-fire means of catapulting the university's reputation, notwithstanding state grumblings over the $76 million cost.

If the commissioning of these starchitect designers is about institutional identity and prestige, money is also a factor. The nomenclature of many of the most dazzling recent forays into iconic campus building reveals the importance of large individual donations to their realization. Gehry's first commission in Australia, for the business school of the University of Technology, Sydney, is titled the Dr Chau Chak

Wing Building in honour of the business leader who donated Aus$20 million towards its construction (see pages 86–9); the Hong Kong Polytechnic University renamed its Zaha Hadid-designed Innovation Tower (2013) to reflect the HK$249 million gifted by the Hong Kong Jockey Club in 2011. 'If you have an exciting building, a Stata Center,' quoted the *Boston Globe* of planning consultant Catherine Donaher, 'you're in a position to say to a prospective donor, "You can have your name on this." People like to be associated with fresh and exciting things, and architecture can be one of them.'[23] The high visibility of big-brand architects brings a significant caché which attracts philanthropists or corporations to attach their name to campus buildings through generous benefactions which typically prove a huge boost to a university's fundraising campaign.

The high price-tags and often spiralling budgets associated with star-status buildings is a common trope. Indeed, the economic crash has prompted a reappraisal of whether 'starchitecture' is a sustainable model for campus building. 'The age of the architectural icon – that extravagant, exuberant, "wow"-inducing building on a pedestal – is dead, or more precisely, in its death throes,' wrote one *Chicago Tribune* critic in 2009 in an article entitled 'Goodbye, icons; hello, infrastructure'. Holl's dormitory at MIT significantly exceeded estimates, some reports say by as much as threefold. Calatrava's YouTube video of his master-planned new campus for the University of South Florida Polytechnic cost $140,000 alone. The future of 'starchitecture' on campuses specifically has been questioned in light of the recession and spending cuts. Prominent projects have been aborted completely whilst others have been delayed, such as Holl's Art and Transit zone at Princeton. Far fewer 'starchitect' projects on campus were completed in the period 2010–3 than in immediately preceding years. Yet a range of high-profile commissions are going ahead, and further examples are being commissioned. In 2012, for example, Monash University in Melbourne and Virginia Commonwealth University in the US unveiled designs for major commissions by Moshe Safdie and Holl respectively.

Opposite above: The Jockey Club Innovation Tower (2013) for the Hong Kong Polytechnic University, Zaha Hadid's first permanent building in Hong Kong.

Opposite below: Virginia Commonwealth University has commissioned Steven Holl to design its new Institute for Contemporary Art.

Next page: In 2012 Monash University invited Moshe Safdie to design the Sir Zelman Cowen School of Music.

SIR ZELMAN COWEN SCHOOL OF MUSIC

Morphosis's extroverted academic building (2009) for Cooper Union.

'Starchitecture' is, moreover, becoming progressively more visible in the campus-scape of nations beyond the West. Institutions here are actively broadcasting their academic aspirations through ambitious, headline-courting structures by international practitioners. The City University of Hong Kong, which gained university status in 1994, opened a Creative Media Centre by Libeskind in 2011; nearby the Hong Kong Polytechnic University, which opened a Hadid-designed tower in 2014, was also given university accreditation in 1994; in 2010 Holl designed an arts centre for Hangzhou Normal University in China, and a year later a doctorate's building for the National University of Colombia in Bogota; while Kuwait University's University City campus (in construction) is an assortment of unique architectural experiments.

University City exemplifies how futuristic flagship buildings are used by new institutions eager to position themselves in a global market. Buildings with the 'wow' factor can prove constructive and immediate tools in building a brand within an evermore-crowded market. Lüneburg's jagged, Libeskind-designed main building is a conclusive instance of a branding exercise being conducted through the vehicle of bricks and mortar. This appetite for buildings as branding has drawn fierce criticism. 'So-called iconic buildings today seem only to represent the iconic intentions of their designers,' one detractor has argued. 'An icon today is a frozen gesture, an unfamiliar form, something strange, different, promoted by media coverage... It is photogenic and its visual qualities can often save it from having to justify itself in terms of functionality, structural coherence and budget.'[24] Context and functionality are valid concerns in any discussion about 'starchitecture', particularly for the university campus where, arguably, these factors are of higher priority than the commercial or civic realm.

Celebrity architecture is by no means antagonistic to good placemaking. Nevertheless, in considering a Gehry building, for instance, our thoughts immediately turn to the sculptural form of its exterior and not, arguably, to the spaces in and around it. By placing a focus on delivering a signature style, 'starchitecture' buildings are liable to forget to respond to the context of their environment. In the US, Thom Mayne's extroverted 2009 building for Cooper Union in New York City, for example, provoked ferocious local opposition for its detachment from the historic Greenwich Village setting the moment plans were published. As soon as the plywood barriers

surrounding it came down, a graffitist registered an unequivocal judgement: 'Aliens! Please park spacecraft elsewhere'.

Avant-garde architecture at its best can engage and energize. It has the potential to embody the ambitions of a university, and inspire the students that experience it for life. It is necessary to remember, though, that a campus is far more than a collection of individual buildings, and exhibitionist structures whether from the office of a celebrity architect or not must consider this sensitive balance. A campus is a place of special resonance, a repository of memories that speaks of the university's missions, values and aspirations. To be successful, starchitecture on campus must not solely be a vehicle for an architect's trademark style; it must advance this culture in a way that is meaningful foremost to the university community.

Striving for innovation and posterity is part and parcel of a university's role as patron, and the prominence of 'starchitecture' at campuses across the world reflects this. Notwithstanding the attention that buildings by the likes of Hadid, Gehry, and Mayne garner, it is important to be mindful that iconic design on campus is not the sole preserve of the celebrity architect nor necessitous of enormous budgets. The Kantana Film and Animation Institute in Thailand, for example, has an eye-catching, sensory building (2011)

SCI-Arc's graduation pavilion by P-A-T-T-E-R-N-S, a tilted, tripartite steel and fabric structure.

delivered at modest scale (one storey, 2,000 square metres/21,500 square feet), by a local architect, in the country's most ubiquitous material – brick. In the US, the Southern California Institute of Architecture's urban campus has embraced the potential of publicity-grabbing building by commissioning a bold 2013 graduation pavilion, but mitigates its risk through the small scale and temporary nature of the project. The structure asserts the institution's reputation for vanguard teaching through a decisive, twisting-box structure scheduled to last only four to five years and costing under $200,000.

Universities have always been places of ambitious patronage and should continue as such. But once the media attention has faded, a building needs to function successfully as a twenty-first-century learning environment, communicating the institutional values within the context of a wider campus setting. In other words, whether authored by starchitects or not, campuses should endeavour to make bold architectural statements but these must be compatible with context and programmatic needs and be adaptable for the future.

HUB BUILDINGS

More than any other of the single-building types profiled in these pages, the hub exemplifies the increased multiflex nature of university life and organization of the last quarter-century. The epithet 'hub' is a term confined largely to the UK, Australia and New Zealand, but it is one which aptly expresses the psyche of the building typology – a single, mixed-used structure intended to be the centre of student activity, both social and academic. The Hub at Coventry University (UK, 2011), for example, has been described by its architect as a 'living room for the whole university'. Under one roof it offers the twenty-first century student a sweeping range of services including a café, dining options, convenience store, medical centre, careers centre, bar, faith centre and informal study zones. Upon opening, it was almost immediately lauded for providing a heart to Coventry's scattered, urban campus. While the building specifics vary from hub to hub, the typology can be broadly defined as a facility that combines provision for recreation and study under one roof, often joined by other student services. The emergence of this trend demonstrates how standard university typologies are evolving to meet new pedagogical approaches and technological advances amidst pressures to attract students in a climate of escalating competition. The origins of the hub type lie in two long-established components of the traditional campus – the library and the student union.

The concept of the student union grew out of the specially erected buildings housing literary or debating societies which first began to appear on American campus in the nineteenth century, such as Phi Kappa Hall at the University of Georgia (1837) and Whig and Cliosophic Halls at Princeton (1837). Over time, this concept broadened. The Harvard Union was constructed in 1900, built not for a particular society but for the whole community as a place to meet and dine. By the 1960s and 70s, student union buildings were integral components of the campus, functioning as social centres of vast proportions, such as the University of Bristol's Queen's Road Building (UK, 1965) which included meeting rooms, television and games rooms, a barber, dining rooms and bars, and swimming pool spread across a floor area equivalent to nearly four football pitches.

Hubs draw their essence from the union's remit of meeting students' pastoral, recreational, and social needs. In fact, several current examples of this trend are renovations and expansions of existing student unions, such as the Goldring Student Centre at Victoria College at the University of Toronto (Canada, 2013). However, hubs have developed the union's role to provide a more integrated, more expansive experience for the student. As well as the bars, dining options, and administration services of the archetypal union, they may offer access to healthcare, counselling, or careers advice. Moreover, they include learning and study options, thus branching into the traditional province of the library.

Tertiary learning methodologies are undergoing continuing re-evaluation. Critically, learning is no longer considered a didactic pursuit confined to the lecture theatre, seminar room, and library. Beginning in the 1990s, changing attitudes towards learning and the application of new technologies prompted a reappraisal

Above: The Ron Cook Hub (BDP, 2010) at the University of York, a gateway building to bring together students, researchers, business and commercial stakeholders, and the wider community.

Opposite: Coventry University's Hub (Hawkins\Brown, 2011) has transformed the commuter campus by providing a 24-hour destination for study, socializing, and student services.

of the longstanding model of the academic library; the result was the emergence of a maturation of this traditional space into a new typology known as 'learning commons', which combined the functions of the library with enhanced IT, expert human support and, moreover, a focus upon collaborative social resources.[25] Spearheaded in the US by institutions such as the University of Southern California and University of Iowa, the genre continues to be popular internationally, as the recent examples at the University of Manchester (2012) in the UK and Tunghai University (2013) in Taiwan suggest.

Learning commons have set a template for facilitating student-orientated experiential learning through collaboration, dialogue, and digital learning which has been assimilated into the new generation of hub buildings. There are significant differences between the two building types, though. Not necessarily linked with a physical library, hubs are more informal in their provision of study spaces and, moreover, they marry these with a host of social, recreational, and support functions that do not feature within the learning commons repertoire. For example, at Edge Hill University in Britain, the Hub (2011) hosts catering outlets, convenience store, and student union offices alongside mixed classroom facilities, IT suites, and individual and group study points. The Coventry Hub fuses its café, bar, and medical surgery with 2,800 square metres (30,000 square feet) allocated to informal study, including 'seating nests' with flat-screen monitors, fulfilling the 'anytime, anywhere' concept of experiential learning.

The division of space between social, learning, and pastoral functions varies from hub to hub. There is no static formula for the building type; indeed, one of its advantages is that the concept carries the flexibility to adapt to the different requirements of different institutions. Some exemplify a greater focus upon academic mission, such as the Nanyang Technological University Learning Hub in Singapore (scheduled for completion in 2014), whilst others such as the Student Centre at the University of the District of Columbia (US, projected to open in 2014) place foremost emphasis upon delivering opportunities for socializing, assembly spaces, and student government offices.

Flexibility, furthermore, is inherent in not only the definition of hub buildings, but is key to their make-up. The ground floor of the Hub at the Victoria University of Wellington (New Zealand, 2013), for instance, was designed with moveable furniture that can be cleared aside to make way for large-scale events. Embodying a trend which is becoming progressively more fundamental to all aspects of campus design, hubs are designed to be versatile in their nature, thus future-proofing themselves against the inevitable changes in university life.

Often branding themselves as 'one stop shops' for student life,[26] the hub typology exemplifies the prevailing emphasis upon consolidating the student experience. Alongside rising tuition fees, expectations are growing and the student is progressively being identified as a consumer. By uniting the core principles of the student experience – teaching, learning, social, support – hubs are perceived as a key means of answering market demands. They are of particular value in the case of dispersed urban campuses with a high proportion of commuter students, such as Coventry University or the University of the District of Columbia whose 6,000-square-metre (65,000-square-foot) Student Centre is anticipated to revitalize campus. The university has not hitherto provided student housing, thus the Student Centre has been commissioned to create a venue that will encourage students not to disperse immediately after class. Furthermore, the hub typology is also being interpreted as a means of impressing prospective high-school pupils through sophisticated modern architecture. Acting as the public face of the University of York's new Heslington East campus, the Ron Cooke Hub (UK, 2010), for instance, is a curving copper-clad volume with floor-to-ceiling glazing overlooking a lake, whose sleek design earned it a nomination for a Royal Institute of British Architects (RIBA) award in 2011.

The commissioning of glossy new hub buildings does not come without long-term risks, nevertheless. Devoting large resources to the student experience as part of the escalating battle for students inevitably diverts scarce funds away from research and faculty appointments, the factors which determine academic reputation. Nonetheless, the amenities arms race is unlikely to abate soon. The provision of consolidated student services and more varied learning settings, accessible around-the-clock in slick new casings, is a trend of sustained importance. As long as this pattern abides, the concept of the hub building will continue to have currency, although its parameters are likely to evolve as new demands, technologies, and pedagogies arise within higher education.

INTERDISCIPLINARY SCIENCE RESEARCH BUILDINGS

The paradigm of the scientist-genius, toiling for years in monastic isolation in pursuit of a breakthrough discovery, has little place in the twenty-first-century world of research universities. Over a decade into the new century, the concept of collaboration across disparate disciplines is becoming ever more prevalent within academia. Epoch-making breakthroughs such as the Human Genome Project have arisen directly from the crossing of scientific boundaries. For the research-intensive university, interdisciplinary practices are opening doors to new areas of teaching and research, and the phenomenon is having tangible impact upon the physical environments of campuses across the globe through the construction of dedicated interdisciplinary science buildings.

Interdisciplinary research is no twenty-first-century invention.[27] Throughout the history of science, spectacular discoveries, new techniques, and new fields have fruited from interdisciplinary intersection. From the days of antiquity – which saw Aristotle embrace an encyclopedic range of subjects from astronomy, to natural sciences, to philosophy – to the discovery of the structure of DNA by James Watson (biologist) and Francis Crick (physicist) alongside Maurice Wilkins (physicist) and Rosalind Franklin (crystallographer), scientific progress has been driven by translational collaboration. Substantially more Nobel Prizes have been awarded for interdisciplinary research than single-discipline research.

Yet, notwithstanding the longstanding role of cross-collaboration in science, the structure of university life has traditionally not been aligned to this approach. The university community has historically been shaped by building blocks of academic departments, each constituting a discrete field of study and each independently controlling recruitment of faculty and programmes of teaching and research. Departments follow their own discrete agendas, creating a culture in which links between departments are loose and rare.[28] The distinctions are not only curricular and social, but also physical; a characteristic university campus is a collection of distinct buildings dedicated to individual departments, schools or colleges. However, since the 1960s, university administrations have gradually become increasingly receptive to the potential for collaborative research.

Inspired by a backdrop of scientific advances across the spectrum, in the 1960s and 70s universities became steadily more aware of the need to keep abreast of cutting-edge research both by establishing new departments and by rethinking the priorities of existing ones. Academia saw new departments of biochemistry, biophysics and genetics spring into being, followed by schools of molecular biology, cell biology, and most recently nanotechnology and bioinformatics. As the potential of translational research became more pronounced and research budgets simultaneously grew, many universities determined that simply expanding departmental facilities was inadequate in the long-term. The concept of the cross-disciplinary research centre, where scientists from a range of fields were brought together to tackle specific topics, was born.[29]

Interdisciplinary research is not therefore a wholly new phenomenon upon the campus, but recent years have seen a new urgency in its implementation as a specific goal. Institutional strategic plans speak time and again of the need 'to stimulate collaboration across subject and faculty borders' (Uppsala University 2008), to 'develop mechanisms to facilitate cross-disciplinary approaches to research' (La Trobe University 2008), of 'interdisciplinarity as a catalyst for innovation' (University of Ottawa 2010). Cross-faculty collaboration is firmly established as a fundamental aspect of achieving world-class status and attracting first-class scholars, encouraged in no mean way by governmental financial incentives.[30]

While interdisciplinary activities can take a number of guises, from the hiring of new faculty to the development of new programmes, recent years have seen a growth in the numbers and significance of the interdisciplinary research centre within capital construction. It is one of the most notable and potentially enduring trends affecting the physical realm of the university today. A survey of campus plans reveals the emphasis being placed upon new physical spaces in the race to explore interdisciplinarity: 'Most critical to Carolina's interdisciplinary goals for excellence is the development of... [new] facilities,' asserted the academic plan of the University of North Carolina at Chapel Hill (USA) for instance. Although costly and difficult undertakings, universities across the world are devoting large resources to the construction of interdisciplinary research institutes.

At the vanguard of the trend as a new building type was Stanford University's James H. Clark Centre (USA, 2003), home of interdisciplinary Bio-X initiative and designed by world-renowned Foster + Partners. Recent examples include the David H. Koch Institute for Integrative Cancer Research (2010) at MIT, the Tyree Energy Technologies Building (2012) at the University of New South Wales in Australia, and the HPL Life Sciences Platform (2013) at ETH Zürich, Switzerland. As the nomenclature of some of these centres imply, private donors are often fundamental to their realization. Universities are also partnering with private foundations and public bodies to create large-scale new facilities, as demonstrated by undertakings such as the Francis Crick Institute in London. When it opens in 2015, the Crick will be an interdisciplinary research super-laboratory bringing together three of the most significant health research organizations – the Medical Research Council, Cancer Research UK and the Wellcome Trust – with three UK universities – University College London, Imperial College London and King's College London – to reignite biomedical research in Britain.

The new buildings vary in shape, size and style, just as the research programmes they contain vary in objectives, activities and structure. Yet certain continuities are in evidence across the spectrum. Architecture and design are engaged to craft buildings with two fundamental characteristics: firstly flexibility, creating facilities that can adapt to changing technology; and secondly, a focus on encouraging new forms of collaboration. Many of the characteristic features were pioneered at the Clark Centre at Stanford.

Unlike traditional laboratory buildings which are broken into many enclosed spaces, interdisciplinary centres place an emphasis on large, shared open laboratories with few walls. The Clark Centre was amongst the first science buildings to embrace this model. Researchers inside the Clark's three wings can look through fully glazed walls into the inner courtyard and across to other laboratories, encouraging cross-team curiosity and visibility. The concept is one of creating 'a window onto science'. In plans for the Francis Crick Institute, architectural practice HOK has attempted something similar by structuring each floor

as four neighbourhoods around a light-filled atrium. The atrium establishes visibility across all floors, HOK has explained. 'If people can't see each other, they aren't likely to meet or collaborate.' The floors will be as open-plan as possible, with partitions being of glass where appropriate, creating a sense of inviting openness amongst the different research groups.

Fostering communication between researchers that would traditionally be housed in different buildings, often in different areas on campus, is a key objective of the interdisciplinary building. Exterior and interior spaces are consciously conceived to nurture interaction between students, faculty and staff. The notion that ideas and activity can be catalyzed by 'chance encounters in the hallway' leads to classrooms, offices, laboratories, and social spaces being deliberately arranged to promote human circulation. At MIT, Ellenzweig Architects had this in mind when they clustered the Koch Institute's common areas – meeting rooms, tearooms, elevators, and bathrooms – together at the centre of the building. At Rockefeller University in New York, the Collaborative Research Centre boasts as its focal point a light-filled elliptical atrium intended as a symbolic realization of the spirit of openness that defines interdisciplinary research. Each aspect of its design was conceived to draw Rockefeller's researchers into collegial interaction. Housing meeting rooms, informal gathering spaces, a café, and lecture theatre, the atrium functions as a hub for the community, facilitating the 'meeting in the corridor' on a large scale.

Alongside collaboration sits the requirement for flexibility. The rapid pace of change in technology and strategies within modern science research makes this quality a necessity. The buildings need to be capable of responding to changing programmatic uses and technological innovations in an economic fashion. Within the Francis Crick Institute, HOK have planned for hubs of strategically-

---

Opposite above: The Clark Centre (2003), Stanford University, was at the forefront of interdisciplinary science architecture, sporting glazed walls and flexible interior.

Opposite below: Main entrance façade of the Francis Crick Institute, designed by lead architects HOK.

Next page: The Francis Crick Institute will be one of the largest single laboratory building in the world when it opens in 2015. Its four storeys are structured around a soaring, naturally-lit atrium.

The Collaborative Research Centre at Rockefeller University (2010), two early twentieth-century laboratories are linked with a contemporary light-filled atrium.

located, fixed core facilities, but these are surrounded by basic laboratories intended to function according to multiple uses. 'There isn't any work space that can't become some other kind of lab,' boasts head designer Bill Odell. 'Even on a floor where we have these core support facilities, if in 10 years the science changes or the technology changes, it can be turned to other uses.' At Stanford's Freidenrich Centre for Translational Research (2012) the two upper floors were designated for clinical trials, and thus had to accommodate regularly changing teams. Architects WRNS Studio created a large, open plan space, avoiding isolated rooms which may be taxing to reconfigure to the fluctuating requirements of the trials. This breed of building is amongst the most challenging of campus structures to design. As critic Paul Goldberger has explained, 'an architect can't decide that he's going to make a wedge-shaped lab just because wedge shapes are his trademark'.[31] Scientists have rigid functional requirements that their research institutes must accommodate. Their design is no easy matter.

As illustrated by the Freidenrich Centre, architects of interdisciplinary research buildings often face the task of designing for sites outside of traditional campus areas. Part of Stanford's School of Medicine, the Freidenrich Centre was planned on parcel-zoned, suburban land. WRNS Studio's brief included that the centre and its forthcoming partner building would form a campus-like presence on this fragmented tract of land that related to the School's main physical identity. The completed building responds to the campus vernacular through its use of terracotta panels, stone-clad arcades, and courtyards, overlooked by first-floor terraces.

As comparatively recent additions to the higher education programme, interdisciplinary buildings frequently find themselves located on campus fringes, entailing the necessity to bridge departments not only intellectually but also physically. The siting of the Koch Institute at MIT demonstrates how, as new research programmes grow, the cumulative effect can be to create new campus districts. The Koch is built to the northeast of MIT's traditional heart in an area that was neglected and obsolete until the late 1990s when the university embarked upon a series of building projects to house its high-technology research programmes. With the construction of the Stata Centre

Cairns Institute (2013) at James Cook University, one of a small number of interdisciplinary buildings designed to stimulate cross-collaboration outside the STEM subjects.

(2004) for information science and technology, the Brain and Cognitive Sciences Complex (2005), the Broad Institute for Genomics (2006), plus the appearance of an adjacent cluster of external biotechnology enterprises on this land, a neighbourhood of high-technology research grew up which has resulted in a new focal point for the university community distinct from its historic core. The design of the Koch Institute, prominently located on the northern boundary of the campus, sought to enhance this effect by creating a significant new campus gateway and the largest new courtyard since MIT's construction a century ago.

The prominence of interdisciplinary research buildings on campus will almost certainly increase in forthcoming years. The metamorphosis towards heterogeneous research still has far to go; many voices contend that academia's transformation has so far been haphazard and narrow-ranged, that the decentralized organization of university life has meant many institutions have embraced the collaborative labels without adapting their disciplinary structure.[32] Yet there is an almost unanimous desire for more inclusive and constructive integration across academic disciplines to foster scientific inquiry. In the challenge to overcome traditional disciplinary boundaries, universities must plan proactively for the future, and the

tangible outcome of this will undoubtedly be more buildings dedicated to nurturing interdisciplinary engagement. The phenomenon has not been confined solely to scientific enterprises. Brown University's Granoff Centre for the Creative Arts (2011), for instance, is an interdisciplinary arts centre within a dramatic zinc architectural form by Diller, Scofidio + Renfro; the Cairns Institute at James Cook University in Australia (2013), designed by Woods Bagot and RPA Architects, is a research hub housing specialists in the social sciences, humanities, law, and business sectors drawn together to examine issues of importance to tropical nations.

Across academia, universities are looking for ways to promote new forms of collaboration, and there is a demand for physical spaces that encourage this by inspiring proximity, interaction, and thus cross-fertilisation. Carefully-considered laboratory architecture can deliver this through open, modular, and flexible buildings structured around shared infrastructure and communal spaces.

JOINT-VENTURE BUILDINGS

With the spectre of budget cuts, rising utility costs, growing enrolment, and pedagogic changes looming over higher education, universities are adopting innovative strategies when it comes to investing in their portfolio of facilities. One such policy is joint-venture buildings. This approach comes in many guises but, essentially, it encompasses some form of shared ownership, tenancy, or management of a physical space between a university and one or more partners.

The concept is wide-ranging, multi-disciplinary, and is born of a variety of motivations. Joint-venture schemes can arise from the collaboration of two or more higher education institutions, such as University Square (2013) in London which creates a hub for Birkbeck University and the University of East London; or they may be a partnership between a university and local community body, as will be the Camrose Performing Arts Centre (scheduled completion 2014), a joint initiative between the City of Camrose, Camrose County and the University of Alberta in Canada; or they may be a product of universities partnering with commercial industry or research institutes, particularly in terms of science or innovation buildings such as the 2013 complex

developed by pharmaceutical giant Pfizer and MIT. Within this spectrum, there are various levels of partnership, from merely sharing the same roof to the full integration of the participating entities.

From the 1950s onwards, universities and industry have co-located to foster research and enterprise. MIT's Tech Square, for example, was founded in 1961, bringing together tenants engaged in computer science research activities. MIT researchers were brought under the same roof as industry peers including Polaroid and IBM. Universities have also historically shared health facilities with healthcare providers, such as the St George's Heathcare NHS Trust and St George's University which have co-located in south London since 1980. Meanwhile, precedents exist for shared library facilities, including the German National Library of Science and Technology which was inaugurated in 1959 at the Leibniz Universität Hannover, whose holdings formed the basis of the original library which is funded by state and federal government.

Above and opposite: University Square Stratford (Make Architects, 2013) is a £33m development that sees the University of East London (UEL) and Birkbeck, University of London, co-locate in a single-building campus. The spatially-versatile building serves UEL students during the day and Birkbeck's evening classes.

The Centre for AgriBioscience (2012), a partnership enterprise of La Trobe University and the Victorian Department of Primary Industries.

Notwithstanding these precedents, the practice is becoming more strategic and more frequent in response to the changing operating conditions and ambitions of higher education institutions. Universities must contend with the pressure to provide cutting-edge teaching, recreational, residential, and research facilities within a straitened economy and swingeing budget cuts. At the same time, the facilities they build must answer changing pedagogical methods as well as reflect the changing mission and perception of the university within academia and beyond. The university is no longer the sequestered realm of yore, remote from the needs and interests of society in pursuit of cloistered knowledge; beginning in the second half of the twentieth century, its mantle has been recast. Institutions of higher education have an accountability and responsibility to the wider community beyond its campus fringes; they are embracing their role in supporting enterprise and knowledge transfer within business and industry thereby contributing to future economic growth; and they are recognising the value of cross-collaboration in progressive scientific research. As this text will explore, this changing mind-set is having tangible impact upon building and planning patterns. One such symptom is the growing number of joint-venture buildings.

The increasing inventory of partnerships that is arising from the current HE context is generating a spectrum of joint venture models. Within this, several key typologies are emerging: science centres, libraries, and industry collaborations; as are a list of key motivating factors that drive the projects: community cohesion, financial management, and interdisciplinary interaction.

For the research university, sharing science facilities offers benefits both economic and interdisciplinary and in several instances this practice crosses paths with the trend for interdisciplinary research buildings. The costs of constructing, equipping and maintaining vanguard laboratory research centres are vast and, for some institutions, prohibitive; joining forces with other universities or institutes can mitigate this expenditure while sowing the seed for collaborative research which is increasingly held to be central to the future of scientific development. The under-construction Francis Crick Institute in London is a prime illustration of this trend, representing a joint venture between three leading universities and three public medical bodies (see pages 28–32). In Australia, La Trobe University has partnered with the Victorian Department of Primary Industries to open AgriBio, the Centre For AgriBioscience (2012), a 30,000-square-metre (325,000-square-feet) research centre for agricultural biosciences designed to strengthen the university's and state's international reputation for

New Horizons (2013), science centre shared by Monash University and CSIRO.

bio protection research and diagnostics. Nearby, in 2013 Monash University and Australia's national science agency, CSIRO, opened a Aus$156 million research and teaching centre designed by Lyons Architects to bring together scientists and engineers from the two institutions.

The advantages of collaborative research are also being exploited within technology and industry sectors. The growing realization within both business and universities of the pivotal part that universities can play in providing high-level skills, a high-quality research base, and a culture of innovation and inquiry has led to increasing numbers of joint facilities. Cases such as the Volkswagen Automotive Innovation Laboratory at Stanford University (2010) exemplify the salient trend of the collaboration of universities and multi-national corporations. The co-location of industry, research and students creates an arena for intermingling which can support knowledge transfer and skills development. This is the aim behind the Advanced Manufacturing Training Centre (UK, 2014), the product of a University of Sheffield-Boeing partnership. The 5,500-square-metre (60,000-square-feet), purpose-built centre aims to provide the next generation of world leading engineers by developing academic and practical skills at levels from apprentice to post-graduate. Designed by Sheffield architects, Bond

Bryan, the building will include two large workshops plus four floors accommodating preparation space, workshops, classrooms, offices, presentation rooms and a refectory.

For universities, such ventures offer access to potential private funding and expensive technology facilities. Moreover, they bring the potential to expand the horizons of students whilst consolidating the continuing relevance of the institutions themselves. Through universities, corporations can gain access to the latest research in their field and innovative employees in the form of students on work placements and graduates. As universities exert themselves to maintain their relevance beyond the ivory tower, building links with enterprise and innovation is becoming an increasing priority to many institutions which is likely to give further impetus to the joint venture trend. This approach is not limited to large multi-nationals, however. Universities are engaging with businesses of all sizes, including new ventures.

In the US, the UMASS Boston Venture Development Centre (2009) is a hi-tech metal and glass structure on the University of Massachusetts campus. A joint undertaking between the university and the Venture

Development Centre, the project is designed for innovators in their very early stage that require small, reasonably-priced laboratory and office space and the need to collaborate with the university's researchers in order to promote exchange of knowledge and commercialization of research. Designed by Sasaki Associates, it is a flexible and adaptable facility featuring collaboration spaces, offices, laboratories, and informal gathering areas.

Incubators, innovation centres, and accelerators could in themselves form a standalone trend within this publication. This type of facility – devoted to assisting early-stage businesses by providing applied research and business counseling – has grown steadily in stature within university construction since the turn of the millennium. Joint-venture delivery has proved a popular means for universities to achieve this type of accommodation, both in coalition with other educational institutions and with industry or municipal partners. In 2013, the UK's University of Huddersfield opened the 3M Buckley Innovation Centre, housed in a converted mill with a glazed, single-storey extension. Its £12-million cost was funded by the combined efforts of the European Regional Development Fund, the local council, and the university itself. Across the Atlantic, meanwhile, Cornell University, Ithaca College, and Tompkins-Cortland Community College announced their collaboration in 2014 to open an incubator to encourage rising entrepreneurs into Ithaca and thereby increase the region's economic activity. Also an example of adaptive reuse, it will be housed in a repurposed 1922 insurance building in the city centre. By providing focal points for entrepreneurial activity, such projects anchor the role that universities play in their communities.

The ideological and physical integration of a university within its community is a motivational force behind many of this generation of co-locational facilities. Such partnership ventures can strive to support the locality not only financially, but also culturally and educationally. The past two decades have seen a growing experimentation in joint-use university-public libraries in countries such as Australia, Germany, Latvia, Sweden, and the USA. In Colorado, one such example serves 70,000 local residents and 6,000 Front Range Community College faculty and staff in a 7,000-square-metre (76,000-square-foot) facility which opened in 1998. The Almedal Library in Sweden, meanwhile, opened in 2001 as a collaboration between the municipality of Gotland and Gotland University.

Offering potential economic, social, and educational boons, such libraries can significantly improve the quality and quantity of collections and operational efficiency. The Hive in Worcester was the UK's first fully-integrated university and local authority library when it opened in 2012 (see pages 128–31). In an age of austerity when local libraries are closing due to public funding, the model represents a pioneering response to the challenge of providing library services. The co-location of services allows the University of Worcester researchers easy access to the county archive and archaeology records, while the public receives expanded opening hours. Yet designing these spaces successfully is complex. University members need to feel they have access to all the academic resources they require in an environment conducive to study, while the public need spaces and services suitable to them. Experience has shown that joint public-university libraries are complex to manage and operate, are particularly demanding of staff, and are vulnerable to operational difficulties or failure.

Examples of shared-use libraries exist beyond the community-university model, as well. At the University of Leeds campus in the UK, is an example of a library partnership between higher education and business. Designed by Broadway Malyan and opened in 2011, the Michael Marks Building was the product of a partnership between the university and the Leeds-born retailer M&S. Clad in a lightweight, bronze-coloured skin, the structure houses M&S's full company archive of more than 70,000 items and includes expansion space for collections from the university library. Construction, development, and service costs were shared between the two clients.

As at Leeds, Worcester, and elsewhere, the creation of shared spaces allows for economic efficiencies and knowledge exchange between disciplines, business, and institutions; such practices are becoming increasingly valued. Nonetheless, to be successful such facilities require careful consideration. Conflicting requirements and cultural differences between the co-locating institutions are issues that need to be addressed from the outset. In the design stage and after, clear agreement about the allocation of, and access to, resources and services is essential to fulfilling partnerships.

NEW UNIVERSITIES
BEYOND THE WEST

For hundreds of years, the sphere of higher education has been predominated over by the West. The top 25 universities in the world belong to western nations, while half of all Nobel Prizes have been awarded to scholars or graduates of just 12 institutions in Europe and North America. But is this supremacy beginning to waver? Over the past two decades, worldwide university enrolment statistics have soared beyond even the most optimistic forecasts. Between 2000 and 2010, the number of adults with a tertiary education rose from 19 per cent to 29. Overwhelmingly, this boom is being driven by developing and emerging nations. According to a 2012 report by the Organization for Economic Cooperation and Development, by the end of the decade 40 per cent of the world's graduates aged 25–34 will come from China and India alone. The US and EU are forecast to generate little more than a quarter.[33]

Extending the access and quality of national higher education is a key governmental priority of emerging countries around the globe. As knowledge is increasingly being regarded as a pivotal factor of economic growth, higher education is perceived as critical to the transition to developed-country status. A robust higher education sector plays a vital role in creating a competitive workforce and fostering tomorrow's political and business leaders, while also preventing 'brain drain'.

The expansion of higher education outside the west is being effected through a multitude of channels. Students continue to go abroad to be educated; extant universities are dramatically increasing capacity, often with a focus on constructing campuses that support traditional 'westernized' undergraduate experiences; distance or online learning is mushrooming rapidly (see pages 60–1); western higher education providers are engaging in international branch campuses and cross-border partnerships (see pages 43–7); and new universities are opening in purpose-built facilities.

The latter is the most complex, and thus the most protracted, avenue that is currently being adopted to meet the escalating demand for tertiary education in countries with inchoate HE systems. The expansion of university provision cannot be met by the construction of new institutions alone. To thereby satisfy predictions would demand construction of three higher education institutions of 40,000 students each week for the next 12 years.[34] Given the financial strictures of governments across the world, not least those of developing markets, the scale of investment entailed means this is unachievable. Nonetheless, the creation of new universities does form part of the path towards the maturation of national higher education systems in these regions; and the natural by-product of this is the construction of whole-cloth campuses. This new generation of campuses is interesting not only for what it tells us about the current patterns of global education; but, moreover, the scale of wholesale campus design renders this as an instructive subject for review.

The herculean costs, not to mention the degree of administrative coordination, required by the establishment of a new tertiary institution is such that for many emerging nations, campus design does not figure high on the priority list. Many schemes currently in progress have little architectural or urban distinction. Fortunately, though, the field is also giving rise to a select band of innovative and ambitious master plans by internationally-renowned practices of the calibre of UN Studio, Foster + Partners, and Snøhetta.

The commissioning of international planners and architects is in itself a token of the international aims of the new institutions themselves. A clear example of this is the King Abdullah University of Science and Technology (KAUST) in Saudi Arabia, an institution focusing solely on graduate education and research in science and technology. Opened in 2009, KAUST was founded with the explicit intention of addressing Saudi Arabia's disappointing position in global higher-education league tables and boosting its reputation in science and technology research. It is, moreover, a university designed to attract international students. Global practice HOK master-planned the site, fusing into the plan both Arabic

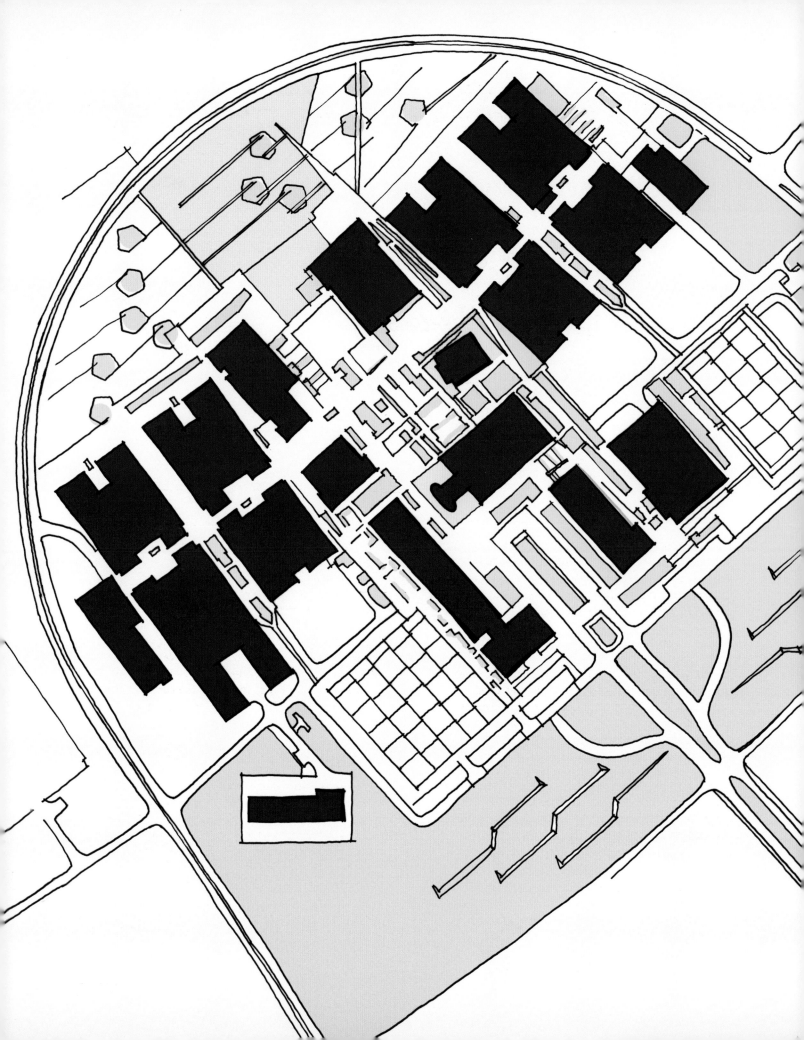

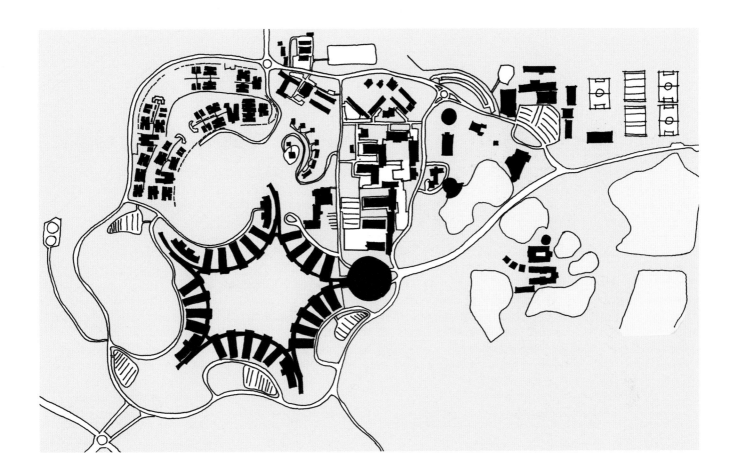

and Western traditions. Arranged in the close-knit formation that characterizes historic Middle Eastern cities, hi-tech buildings house the university's programmes. Indicative of KAUST's tall aspirations, the 1,400-hectare (3,500-acre) campus was designed and built in only 30 months. Few universities have sufficient funding to achieve this kind of pace, however.

In Malaysia, Foster + Partners was selected to master plan the new University of Technology Petronas, completed in 2004 on a 450-hectare (1,100-acre) plot. The university constituted a significant element in the government's plan to become a developed nation by 2020. The institution was established with the clear objective of producing a new generation of technically-qualified, well-rounded graduates capable of contributing to Malaysia's industrial development. It was critical for the university to possess a physical setting that presented an image compatible with these

visionary aspirations. Foster + Partner's master plan arranges the core academic buildings on a radial plan, forming five 'crescents' that surround a central landscaped park. The layout recalls a tropical translation of the age-old quadrangle format, in which cover from the excesses of the sun and rain was provided by an all-encompassing canopy supported by tall, slender columns. Development followed the contours of the ground, with the star-shaped structure wrapped around the curves of the land and enclosing jungle-like parkland, natural to the terrain.

Fully funded by the oil giant Petronas, the University of Technology Petronas is one of a new breed of company-sponsored universities. In Hanoi, a state-owned oil and gas company that accounts for 20 per cent of Vietnam's GDP – PetroVietnam – is currently constructing PetroVietnam University (phase 1 scheduled to be completed in 2016). New Zealand architects Brewer Davidson in conjunction with Australian practice Norman Day and Associates won a design competition for the campus, with a master plan that mediates western campus planning methods with local styles. Campus buildings are organized

Above: University of Technology Petronas (2004) in Malaysia, master planned by Foster + Partners.

Opposite: King Abdullah University of Science and Technology (KAUST) in Saudi Arabia opened in 2009 to a master plan by HOK.

in quadrangles with interior courtyards set within the natural framework of rolling hills. Brick was recommended as the dominant material to echo the natural rich-red colour of the local soil.

Sited on a 175-hectare (430-acre) greenfield site near Noi Bai international airport, PetroVietnam University illustrates the importance of a strategic location for these new universities. Designed to attract foreign investors and participation and to present the campus as a node of a global network, new universities often seek sites close to airport and business hubs. Another such example is the Singapore University of Technology and Design (SUTD), currently in construction (see pages 142–5). Crucially located between Changi airport and Changi Business Park, the new institution is being lauded as the fourth and most prestigious university within Singapore's growing higher education ambit. Its ambitions are reflected in its master plan, commissioned from cutting-edge, Amsterdam-based practice UNStudio, whose portfolio consists of the award-winning Mercedes-Benz Museum in Stuttgart and Music Theatre in Graz. When completed, the campus will be structured around two main axes: a living and a learning spine which overlap at a central plaza to form the university's geographical and interactional heart. Green roofs are incorporated throughout to offer additional outdoor space.

The trend for ambitious whole-cloth master plans is most prolific in, but has not been limited to, the Middle and Far East alone. Africa has a nominal presence within global HE, but new institutions are being founded to address an acute shortage of universities in some parts of the continent. In 2009, Norwegian architects Snøhetta unveiled a master plan for the University of the Gambia which, although founded in 1999, had been operating in borrowed premises. In 2010, American practice Hanbury Evans Wright Vlattas + Company won first place in a competition to master plan the Angola Central Highlands University, a private institution in the Bié province spanning 3,100 hectares (7,700 acres) sponsored by the American charity SHAREcircle. As a region, meanwhile, Latin America is undergoing an important

transformation in its higher education provision. Levels of participation have increased significantly over recent years, resulting in the creation of new institutions, such as the University of Engineering and Technology (UTEC) in Peru which achieved university status in 2011. A campus is currently under construction in Lima, master-planned by Dublin-based Grafton Architects who have envisioned the restricted site as a man-made cliff of cascading volumes.

Tertiary education is high on the agenda in India, meanwhile. The country is grappling with the problem of how to skill an enormous population, over 500 million of which is under 25, in order to sustain its economic growth. To meet the growing need – and hunger – for higher education, the government plans to increase India's student capacity by an extra 10 million by 2017. Such a target is unattainable without the establishment of new institutions, and several are underway. Construction is ongoing, for example, at the residential campus of Ashoka University in Haryana, championed by its founders as India's first Ivy League-standard liberal arts college. Likewise the Central University of Tamil Nadu is being built in phases upon a 210-hectare (515-acre) site in the Cauvery Delta region for a target population of 10,000. Its master plan, produced by Space Matrix and BLINK Design Group, incorporates natural ventilation, rainwater harvesting, and solar energy to minimize stress on the surrounding ecology, while its buildings employ local stone and fly ash, an industrial corollary of thermal power plants. Aspiring to meet the highest criteria of the national green building evaluation system, it is being dubbed as India's first ecological university campus.

While the West still controls global HE policies, practices, and ranking tables, there is a consensus that emerging-market universities will grow in numbers, size, and prominence. Enormously costly and laborious to realize they may be, but as governments progressively prioritize the creation of knowledge economies the inauguration of new universities is likely to feature on national agendas. The scope and design ambition of several current examples whets the appetite for the future.

TRANSNATIONAL EDUCATION

The main entrance of the Texas A&M Engineering building (2007) within Doha's vast Education City (Hamad Bin Khalifa University).

Students have been travelling abroad for a university education since the Middle Ages; more recently, however, a new alternative has emerged: the university is travelling abroad to them. In response to a host of factors – a more integrated world economy, improved travel and communications, aggrandizing of national policies – the sphere of higher education is internationalizing, and becoming an increasing part of the global market place. The most visible manifestation of this is transnational education, by which is meant education provision from one country offered in another. It can take the form of a wide matrix of activities, including franchises, validation, partnerships, and international branch campuses (IBCs). Of these, it is IBCs and partnerships that have relevance to a discussion about academia's built environment.

Loosely defined as an offshore operation of an HEI with a physical presence that grants degrees validated by the parent institution, IBCs are not a brand new phenomenon. The US's Temple University and Georgia Tech University have maintained outposts respectively in Tokyo and France

since 1982 and 1990. Yet over the past decade, media and scholarly interest in overseas satellites has boomed.

Much of this is driven by the increasingly ambitious aims of Middle and Far Eastern governments for national higher education provision. Traditionally, IBCs have been dominated by a 'North to South' movement, in which Anglophone nations have exported their model outside the global West. The Middle East has been a dominant host region, boasting 25 per cent of the world share of IBCs in 2009, although the centre of gravity is progressively shifting eastwards. The activity belongs to wider political stratagems, often associated with plans to establish a knowledge and service-based economy. The most high-profile examples tend to be those located within 'education hubs', which embody planned government initiatives to build concentrated nerve centres of learning. Dubai International Academic City, for example, opened in 2007 as part of the emirate's goal to secure a future beyond fossil fuels as a regional focus for education and enterprise. On a 170-hectare (415 acres) site, 21 HEIs rent space within its collection of sand-coloured building

groups, making it the largest concentration of branch campuses anywhere in the world. A Malaysian counterpart, EduCity, is in development after the government singled out higher education as one of its prime strategic investments to boost local pools of skilled workers as part of long-term goals to foster economic growth. It will eventually house eight individual campuses plus shared sports, residential, and other student facilities.

There is no single model for the type of campus that these satellite outposts assume. Indeed, the term international branch 'campus' is misleading since often the institution operates from a few rented rooms.[35] A 2011 survey of IBCs recorded that 28 per cent of home institutions wholly owned their campus, 18 per cent leased premises, while in the remaining 54 per cent of cases facilities were constructed and owned by local governments or private partners.[36] Within this spectrum of ownership, is a spectrum of size and architectural ambitions.

Doha's vast 1,000-hectare (2,500-acre) hub, Education City (renamed Hamad Bin Khalifa University in 2011 in honour of Qatar's emir), sits at the higher reaches of this scale. Conceived as an architectural mixing pot of eye-catching buildings by a roster of leading international architects, it was master planned by RIBA Gold Medal-winning Japanese architect Arata Isozaki. Spread across a site over four times bigger than New York's Central Park, its collection of lavish facilities hosts satellite offerings from Carnegie Mellon, Texas A&M, and HEC Paris amongst others. Texas A&M's engineering school is housed within a two-wing building measuring 55,000 square metres (592,000 square feet), designed by renowned Mexican firm Legoretta + Legoretta, who are also responsible for a 2011 student centre; Antoine Predock is responsible for a 32,500-square-metre (350,000-square-feet) venue for Northwestern University, whose limestone exterior is modelled upon natural desert foundations; while OMA have prepared plans for three structures, including the 40,000-square-metre (425,000-square-foot) futuristic Central Library. Given that in 2011, the hub graduated only 243 students across all institutions, the scale of the spaces is enormous.[37]

Education City typifies a common approach to IBC construction in that the home institutions do not act as

clients and there is little design kinship between the original campus and its satellite confrère. Education City's member universities played scant, if any, part in the aesthetics of their buildings; instead this role was ascribed to the Qatar Foundation. The non-profit foundation is the force behind the project. Chaired by the emir's wife, Sheikha Mozah Bint Nasser al-Missned, its prime purpose is to expand and fortify education within Qatar, preparing the nation's economy for the post-oil era. The foundation has cherry-picked a variety of schools, inviting them to offer programmes in which they specialize, typically upon a 10-year contract.[38] The foundation finances all running costs, and also presides over physical design choices.

Similarly, the design of the Malaysian campus of Scotland-based Heriot-Watt University (due to open 2014) is controlled by Putrajaya Holdings Sdn Bhd, the company behind the delivery of the project. Located on a 2.5-hectare (six-acre) waterfront site, the complex is on a 25-year lease to the university. The £35-million purpose-built property is being branded as a 'green campus', housing educational facilities and commercial outlets within a state-of-the-art sustainable block capped by a landmark curved green roof.

Examples of home institutions playing the direct patron on IBCs are rare as a consequence of the patterns of ownership. Yet they can be found. The 44-hectare (110-acre) New York University-Abu Dhabi campus (scheduled to open in 2014) designed by Rafael Vinoly makes for one such example of this upon a large scale. Likewise in EduCity, the UK's University of Reading is acting as client for its forthcoming branch campus being designed by Scott Brownrigg and Gillespies. Scheduled to open in 2015, the 2,000-student site will see departmental blocks grouped around a covered, landscaped atrium.

Fuelled by images of glossy renderings and tropical climes, such projects are a magnet for media attention. Yet the future of IBC development as a long-term trend is held in doubt. Several prominent examples are being planned – many revealing a growing 'South to South' migration, such as Xiamen University's plans to open the world's largest branch campus in Malaysia, funded by the China Development Bank. Nevertheless, there have been sundry high-profile closures, cancellations, and delays. Suffolk University (based in Boston, USA) closed its Senegal outpost in 2011 after sustaining considerable financial losses on the 12-year project; while New York University's Tisch School of the Arts Asia in Singapore is billed for closure in 2015.

Opposite: A shaded walkway within the ceremonial court of Education City, Doha, designed by Arata Isozaki.

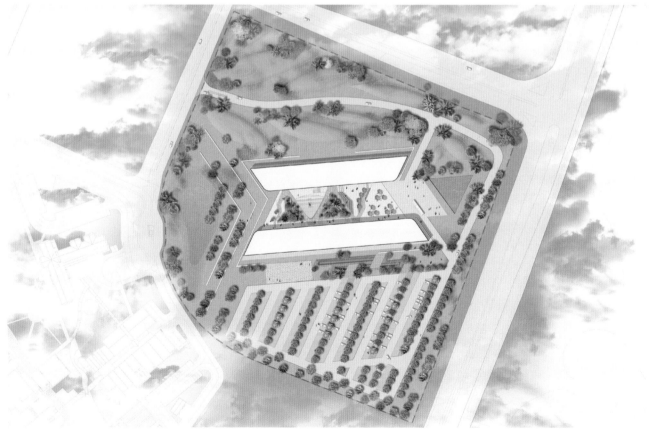

Arguably, partnership ventures are gaining ground as a transnational alternative to bona fide IBCs. Several major institutions are following this route, in which a foreign university partners with a domestic counterpart to form a standalone institution. As the focus shifts to Asia, this mechanism is likely to proliferate. In two of the most important markets for higher education, China and India, overseas universities presently cannot legally establish an independent campus but must ally with a local institution.

Such partnerships are yielding some of the most-anticipated master plans in the field of academic architecture. The UK-China alliance of the University of Liverpool and Xi'an Jiaotong University has resulted in the first independent Sino-foreign university in China, with a 100-acre (40-hectare) campus master plan designed by global practice Perkins + Will (see pages 160–3). The union is a recognition of the emergence of China as an increasingly prominent actor in science and technology and its growing commitment to augment its higher education offering; in partnering with the C9 university, Liverpool has made a proactive step to harness this burgeoning market. Meanwhile, US-based Ivy-League Yale is embarking upon a highly-publicized collaboration with the National University of Singapore (NUS), to create an autonomous, fully-residential college in Singapore (see pages 152–5). The objective of the undertaking, christened Yale-NUS, is to introduce a broad-based, liberal-arts style undergraduate education to the island nation thereby broadening its educational ambit and cementing its reputation as a regional academic hub for Asia. Its campus design – authored by Pelli Clarke Pelli Architects with Forum Architects – brings a tropical twist to the type of quadrangular layout that characterizes Yale's home campus. Colonnades and overhanging eaves protect from Singapore's extremes of rain and sun, 'skygardens' provide high-rise patios dotted amongst its collegiate towers, and native flora provide natural shade.

Meanwhile, the partnership venture between Cornell University and the Technion-Israel Institute of Technology is generating an aura of excitement among architectural circles. Cornell Tech, as the initiative is known, unites

the prestigious US school with the Haifa-based research university to form a science and engineering hub (see pages 156–9). It will offer jointly-awarded degrees from a five-hectare (12.5-acre) base in New York City. Numerous practitioners of note are contributing to its plan, architecture, and landscape, which boasts extensive open-space provision, connected vistas to the Manhattan skyline, and aspirations for net-zero energy use.

At first glance, the coalition of Cornell and Technion in Manhattan may appear unexpected; nonetheless the marriage is a strategic one, programmed to answer a global call from the city's mayor to found a new campus that will boost New York City's participation in the applied sciences and, in so doing, enrich its economy. Technion, with a curriculum focused on science, engineering, and medicine, has long been lauded as the driving force behind one of the world's most thriving high-tech business zones surrounding its Haifa campus. Cornell has engineering and computer science programmes that rank in the US top ten.

Cornell Tech demonstrates a common feature of transnational partnership institutions, in that the overseas party does not bear the capital costs for the venture, thereby diminishing financial risk. The same applies to Xi'an Jiaotong-Liverpool University and Yale-NUS. However, the activity is not without its risk. Fuelled by concerns about academic freedom, one Yale faculty member has dubbed the Singapore venture 'Frankenyale'. The denunciation reflects fears amongst a faction of its members that it is diluting its values by selling its brand to a nation whose government wields heavy restrictions on public speech and assembly. The pairing of Cornell with Technion has similarly provoked controversy on political grounds, with some students and staff questioning the latter's involvement in the Israeli military-industrial complex and major defense corporations.

Transnational campuses are still an unproven model for the long-term. In the grand catalogue of university capital construction such projects are firmly in the minority, yet they are producing some innovative responses to large-scale, whole-cloth design for twenty-first-century education. The increasing numbers of strategic research alliances that are being forged across continents within academia suggests that transnational partnerships will be a dynamic instrument within global higher education markets in future years. How this translates in physical terms to the built environment of higher education is sure to evolve in the decades to come.

Opposite above: The first phase of Heriot-Watt University's branch campus in Malaysia is projected to open in 2014.

Opposite below: The University of Reading-Malaysia campus is set to open in 2015. Its master plan groups department buildings around a semi-external 'heart'.

COMMERCIAL DEVELOPMENTS

The millennium-long history of the university is a narrative dogged with tales of 'endemic border warfare' between universities and their surroundings.[39] From the birth of the university as an institution, the two sides of town and gown have shared a relationship as antagonistic as it is symbiotic. For much of its history, the university has seen itself as an enclave, an introspective and reflective community of scholars removed from the demands and distractions of modern life. Increasingly, however, this persona is fading; in its place comes a far more synergetic outlook, one that considers the university *of*, not simply *in* the city.[40] Universities are increasingly aware of the importance of their urban fabric, and are making moves towards better integration within the city.

Recent years have seen universities become increasingly interested in the area around their campuses. Since the 1990s, when the University of Pennsylvania initiated a series of interventions in its insalubrious West Philadelphia surroundings that included improved street lighting, retail development, and landscaping, a range of institutions have undertaken campus-edge developments.[41] Particularly in North America, but also emerging within other Anglophone nations, a new phenomenon has arisen: the university as urban developer. It is, as one commentator has described it, a case of enlightened self-interest. Universities are fundamentally place-based institutions; while corporations or retail stores can leave a city with relative ease, very rarely are universities able, or motivated, to relocate. Since they are effectively tied to their immediate setting, universities have a strong interest in improving their campus environs.

Universities have historically acted as large-scale commercial landowners in the towns they inhabit. The University of Michigan in the US, for example, owns 22 per cent of downtown Ann Arbor. However, more and more institutions are assuming a new role by using these land holdings to create urban neighbourhoods and large-scale mixed-use developments which are outside of, or peripheral to, their academic remit.

Given the uncertainties of future university funding, a mixed-use project can make for an attractive entrepreneurial opportunity. However, overwhelmingly what characterizes this trend is not profit-making but place-making. At the heart of the phenomenon of universities as urban designers is a drive to create high-quality, enduring, and walkable communities. Aware of the responsibility they have to their members and urban neighbours over the short and long haul, universities envisage these projects in terms of creating a legacy rather than short-term financial gain. These are long-range schemes, indicative of a university's investment in the future of its region.

There is a dual rationale behind this emphasis on place-making. Both the campus and its vicinity play an important part in shaping the campus experience. In a crowded higher education marketplace, the best students and faculty are enticed not only by academic reputations but also by calibre of environment. Improving vibrancy, safety, and aesthetics in and around its grounds can give an institution the competitive advantage.

This reasoning has prompted several recently-completed and in-progress schemes. In the US, for instance, the Gateway project at the University of Toledo, known as a commuter school, was an initiative to build a sense of unity by enticing more students to its environs and keeping them there for longer. Likewise, Storrs Center is a development instigated by a coalition including the University of Connecticut adjacent to its campus that attempts to make up for the perceived lack of a college-town ambience in Mansfield. Containing 15,000 square metres (160,000 square feet) of shops and restaurants, 2,800 square metres (30,000 square feet) of office space, 650 residential units marketed towards young professionals, university staff, and empty nesters, and open green space, the district is intended to boost the amenities of Mansfield, thus enhancing the university's draw to prospective students.

Unlike Storrs Center, Discovery Rise at James Cook University in Cairns is a project that will redevelop a portion of land within the existing campus boundary into a mixed-use community (see pages 174–7). However, it shares the goal of augmenting and intensifying the

campus experience in order to boost the institution's appeal. Incorporating academic, social, artistic, and commercial facilities, the 60-hectare (148-acre) site will be a 'living-learning' community that blurs the boundary between the university and neighbouring Townsville. 'As you drive through the campus,' the project's director envisions, 'you're never quite sure if you're in the university or part of the city, because we will be engaged with the community.'

In this emphasis on the surrounding community lies the secondary half of the rationale behind the importance attached to place-making. The street-friendly, new urbanist planning and architecture of schemes such as the Ohio State University's South Campus Gateway (USA, 2005) mark a sea change from attitudes in the 1960s and 70s, when US institutions in particular cleared entire urban blocks to build single-purpose academic buildings. Universities are increasingly recognizing their contribution and responsibilities to the communities in which they are based. As major contributors to the economic health and physical landscape of cities, universities have come to harness real estate development as part of the community development process.[42]

In broad terms, this trend can be categorized using three typologies: type, scale, and degree of integration with academic mission. Three general 'types' exist. First, are the greenfield types, those projects that are built on hitherto undeveloped land such as the proposed North West Cambridge expansion (see pages 170–3) or UniverCity at Simon Fraser University in Vancouver, Canada, a settlement located adjacent to a commuter campus with a projected population of 10,000 (construction commenced 2002). Second, are brownfield developments which encompass mixed-use construction within campus boundaries or, more frequently, at the outskirts of campuses. After purchasing 10 hectares (25 acres) of declining commercial property at the gateway of its campus, Notre Dame University (Indiana, USA) for example worked with private developers to create a $215 million mixed-use complex of housing, retail, hotel, and office components christened the Eddy Street Commons (2010). With such examples, the physical edges of campus are increasingly becoming blurred within their

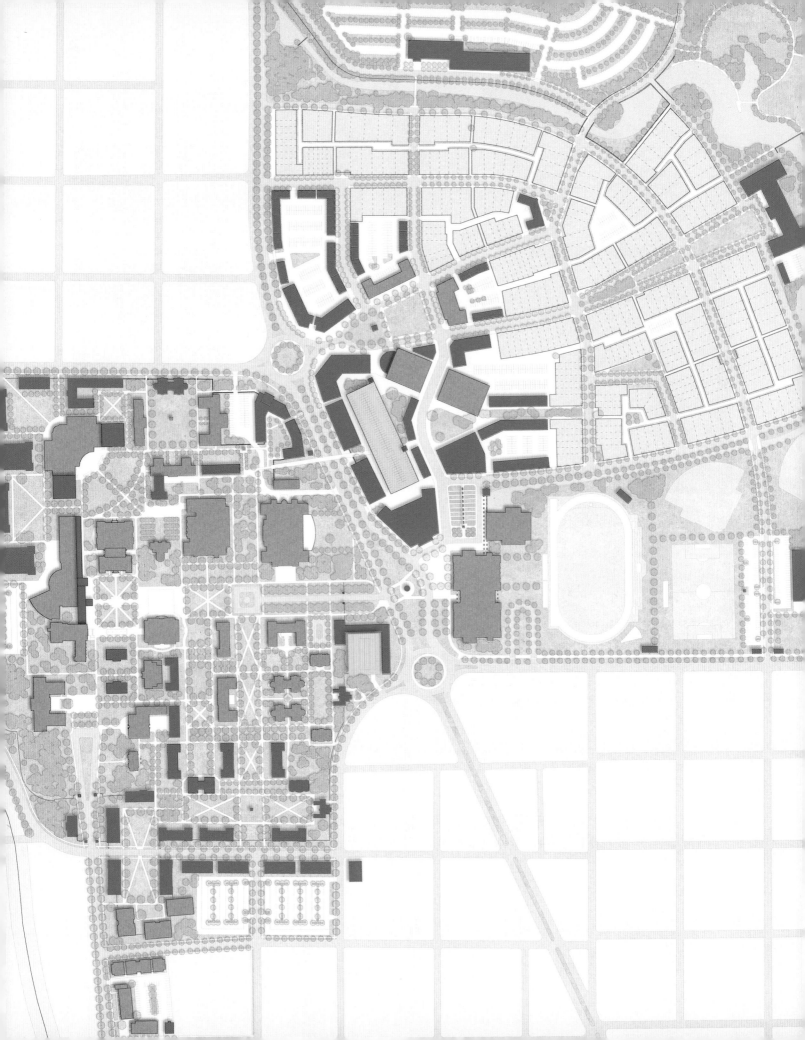

urban fabric. Thirdly, at the lowest investment end of the spectrum, are the types of soft intervention that the University of Pennsylvania began with in the mid 1990s, actions such as improving street furniture, landscapes, and community outreach programmes.

The undertakings, furthermore, vary in scale. North West Cambridge represents the trend at its most ambitious. Projected to cost £1 billion, the site extends over 150 hectares (370 acres) and will see market housing, student accommodation, retail, a primary school, academic and commercial research facilities, and supporting services built in phased stages. Projects this expansive are, nonetheless, rare. Mid-scale instances include Hendrix College (Arkansas, USA), which used 38 hectares (93 acres) of adjacent sports fields to create The Village at Hendrix, a New Urbanist community, commenced in 2004. At the furthest end of the hierarchy, in 2012 the University of Toledo in Ohio completed a mixed-use gateway development of retail and accommodation comprised of a total of only 7,500 square metres (81,000 square feet).

The degree of integration with academic mission – the final defining typology – can simply be registered in terms of the extent to which the urban developments accommodate university functions. This varies in scale. Often, there is no crossover, as at Simon Fraser's UniverCity or Notre Dame's Eddy Street Commons. The East Campus Gateway, a brownfield development by the University of Wisconsin–Madison (USA), is primarily a retail and apartment building offering, yet does include a nine-storey Student Services Tower (see pages 166–9). At the highest end of the register, the North West Cambridge master plan uses market housing to offset the cost of academic facilities and collegiate accommodation required to meet the university's long-term growth needs.

Growing numbers of colleges are working with local government, developers, and lenders to deliver the mixed-use projects. In Australia, since the late 1990s, Queensland University of Technology (QUT) has been working in partnership with the Queensland Department of Housing to develop a 16-hectare (40-acre) brownfield parcel of inner Brisbane surrounding the academic campus to create Kelvin Grove Urban Village. The concept – a mixed-use district combining university facilities, different housing types, retail and leisure activities – was then a radical idea in the context of Australian higher education. At a time when many other Australian institutions were pursuing plans to diversify and establish satellite campuses, QUT's strategy was to focus on enhancing the on-campus experience for its members. With a master plan by HASSELL (2000) based on sustainable 'urban village' design principles drawn from UK practice, construction began in 2002. Throughout its actualization, the village has been extolled as an exemplar in forming new approaches to urban master planning and development. Although the Department of Housing and QUT embarked upon the venture with different goals – respectively to augment its affordable housing provision and to gain a competitive advantage through an urbanized campus experience – their dual commitment to creating an open, permeable plan engendered a high level of consensus within the partnership.[43]

Such partnerships can yield transformative effects upon towns and cities. Tacoma in Washington, USA, is one such success story. In 1997, the University of Washington, Tacoma opened in a former warehouse in a historically industrial but by then decayed area bereft of economic investment and people. The partnering of the university with local and state government and businesses resulted in a mixed-use overhaul of the area that has proven instrumental in energizing regeneration in other underutilized neighbourhoods of the city. The university blends fluidly into its urban backdrop, with most campus buildings having ground-floor retail.

Fusing both the requirements of the academic community and those of the city, the role of the university as urban designer is a composite and challenging one. Precedents such as the University of Washington, Tacoma, though, illustrate that the approach can thrive. The demands made upon the physical campus are evolving, and this trend demonstrates how universities are moving forward to reflect the new needs of the communities – both scholarly and urban – that study, work, reside, and experience the campus and its immediate environs.

Opposite: Hendrix College is creating a new community adjoining its campus. The Village, master planned by DPZ, is sited on the northeast section of the plan, and is now in its third phase of development.

LARGE-SCALE CAMPUS EXPANSIONS

Notwithstanding the repeated references to tightened budgets, shrinking government funding, and reduced endowments that have accompanied the global recession, one of the most remarked-upon phenomena of the twenty-first-century higher-education landscape is large-scale, high-profile expansion projects. In 2007, Harvard released plans for a 100-hectare (250-acre) expansion into neighbouring Allston; Russia's National University Science and Technology is currently building a 40-hectare (100-acre) campus in Moscow designed by Mecanoo; while the University of Oxford is expanding onto a recently-acquired 4.25-hectare (10.5-acre) site in the city centre, known as the Radcliffe Observatory Quarter.

The trend belongs to the global growth of the higher education field. In China, in particular, universities both prestigious and up-and-coming are rapidly expanding their existing facilities to accommodate many times their intended number of students. Chengdu University of Technology is building a 133-hectare (330-acre) extension around its present campus; in 2011 Fudan University in Shanghai commissioned the Miralles Tagliabue studio to master plan a School of Management (in progress) – its fifth campus – to meet a growing demand for MBA places; and Shandong University is constructing a new campus for 25,000 students, due for completion in 2016. Both Shandong and Fudan feature on the list of institutions that have been allocated significant extra funding under Project 985, a Ministry of Education initiative to procure a body of elite, world-status universities.

The pattern of large-scale university expansions is a symptom of the factors shaping the industry. At the simplest level, enrolments are growing and more students require a bigger built footprint. In the US, for instance, Fordham University commenced construction in 2011 of a long-range expansion set to add 230,000 square metres (2.47 million square feet) to its Manhattan campus, which currently measures 74,000 square metres (790,000 square feet). In the same city, Columbia University's seven-hectare (17-acre) Manhattanville addition will see the institution's size grow by over a third (see pages 184–7). At a strategic level, HEIs are sustaining greater participation within STEM research and commercial innovation as part of a wider bias currently being pursued by national governments, resulting in a swath of development devoted to these disciplines. For example, Shandong's new site will house its Engineering College; and Swansea University in the UK is building a 69-acre (28-hectare) Science and Innovation Campus (begun 2013, Hopkins Architects).

Aside from statistical and strategic changes, the trend for large-scale expansion is also illustrating something very interesting about how the university perceives itself and its mission, specifically in terms of the wider world beyond the academic bubble. The 'campus experience' remains a compelling ideal; however, the historic concept of the campus as an enclave is no longer considered prudent for the twenty-first century. Universities are deliberately seeking closer integration with and approximation to urban life. As explored briefly earlier, in the late twentieth century universities began to awake to and respond to their own role in the cultural, economic, and social development of their host city. Today, universities are increasingly active within their own communities. The large-scale expansions that they are undertaking frequently transcend the immediate institutional requirements to encompass wider urban amenities and engagement. The approach is not solely civic-minded, though. It is also reflective of the continual battle to deliver the finest student experience that will set an institution apart from its peers. Students want to be in campus settings that have the energy and resources of an urban centre; they want their campuses to be like cities. The 'city' has thus become a driving force in shaping the physical and programmatic form of the university environment.

The current generation of expansion projects – in the West at least – have turned their back upon the introverted, exclusionary campus compounds of the past, and to a growing extent are demonstrating porosity and interconnection with their surroundings. The contrast between Columbia's 1890s Morningside Heights campus and its in-progress construction, Manhattanville, is a case in point. While the original is enclosed by a tall, bastion-like perimeter that effectively creates an academic island within Morningside Heights, the new campus is designed to allow the street grid to permeate the campus, to provide generous public open space, and to purpose ground floors for commercial uses to encourage pedestrian activity.

Opposite: Shandong University's new campus covering 200 hectares (500 acres) has been master planned by Perkins Eastman.

More and more universities are referencing their desire to respond and contribute to urban life within their mission statements. A glance across the list of large-scale expansions recently completed and currently in progress reveals that many of these projects are being driven by aspirations to consolidate scattered or suburban campuses into inner-city buildings. In 2011, Sasaki Associates prepared a new campus master plan to bring together the scattered facilities of the Universidad del Istmo in Guatemala for the first time on a single campus. In Austria in 2013, the Wirtschaftsuniversität Wien completed a £142-million campus which unites its departments hitherto dispersed across Vienna in the upwardly-mobile Leopoldstadt district. In Britain, Birmingham City University is undertaking a phased removal from eight campuses to two new principal sites on the city-centre's eastern edge, where there is a wider regeneration project to create a learning quarter.

Such moves will bring greater operational efficiency and will intensify the spatial experience for its members, but they are also evidence of the aspirations of HEIs to contribute to cultural and economic regeneration within their cities. In 2012, for example, the UK's University of Ulster submitted a planning application for a £250-million expansion – the largest investment in the institution's history – in inner-city Belfast to enable the relocation of suburban facilities (see pages 180–3). The Greater Belfast Development is being heralded as a dynamic new chapter, not only for the university but also in the life of the city and region. The project will see the construction of three new buildings, substantially glazed and with lower storeys accessible to the public to blur the boundaries between academic and urban realms. The Vice-Chancellor has stressed that the university is 'anxious to ensure that the entire city and province benefits economically, socially, and culturally from the development – especially those communities bordering our campus. This will be an open and accessible campus without iron gates or surrounding walls.'[44] In particular, the university has stressed the regenerative benefits of the scheme by stimulating economic development in a hitherto-forgotten corner of Belfast. The venture sits alongside a spectrum of neighbouring public and private schemes intended to regenerate that section of the city.

Large-scale university expansion projects are carrying strong hopes for the rejuvenation of urban districts across the globe. In 2013 Israel's Bezalel Academy of Art and Design unveiled their plans to relocate to downtown Jerusalem (designed by Pritzer-Prize winning SANAA, scheduled completion 2017). The move has been lauded by the city's mayor as an 'historic turning point in the cultural renaissance' of the city. Similarly, the current expansion of the UK's Manchester Metropolitan University to create a new home for the faculties of education and health, psychology, and social care is being invoked as a significant vehicle for furthering the regeneration of Hulme, an inner-city ward of Manchester which has been a target of government revitalization efforts since the 1990s. The Birley Fields campus, master planned by Sheppard Robson and due to open in 2014, will combine teaching, office, research, and accommodation facilities with 42,000 square metres (450,000 square feet) of new public urban realm. Plans, moreover, include an integrated healthcare service for students and local residents, shared community sports hall, and performing arts studio.

Yet notwithstanding the maxims of shared facilities, public outdoor space, and porosity of plan, university expansions at this large scale in urban precincts are inevitably contentious. When Manchester Metropolitan announced their plans for Birley Fields, local residents immediately cited fears of excess traffic, the loss of open space, and bemoaned the poor consultation process. In Manhattan, meanwhile, expansion proposals submitted in 2012 by New York University for nearly 60 acres (23 hectares) of additional academic and residential space in historic Greenwich Village have generated vitriolic censure from residents, students, and faculty for their scale, expense, and bullish nature. Nearby, Columbia has faced a well-publicized battle with community groups to realize its Manhattanville scheme, centred largely upon the controversial eminent domain strategy which the university employed to acquire some of the required land. Various measures have been taken to ease the university's relations with its neighbours, notably a $76 million fund allotted to community programmes and an emphasis on outdoor public realm within the master plan.

Challenges notwithstanding, large-scale expansion is an important global trend particularly within research-intensive institutions. And it is one that will persist, impelled by rising enrolments and needs to fortify STEM and research facilities. What is more, its continuation will bring new physical expressions of the complex, challenging but symbiotic relationship between town and gown in twenty-first-century society.

Opposite: The new hillside campus of the Universidad del Istmo will consolidate its scattered buildings and enable its student population to increase.

18

16

8

9

15

2

17

7

4

3

1

10

6

5

11

12

11

12

13

14

1. Student Centre
2. Library
3. Rectory
4. Campus Plaza
5. Amphitheatre
6. University Chapel
7. Health School
8. Business School
9. Education School
10. Engineering School
11. Design School
12. Law School
13. Sports Centre
14. Student Housing
15. University Hospital
16. Future R&D
17. Drop Off Plaza
18. Sports Field

REVITALIZING MASTER PLANS

University leaders and administrators face a constant campaign to ensure that their institution is meeting the demands of twenty-first-century education. Advances in pedagogy and technology, growing enrolments, and consumer expectations must all be accommodated within the bricks and mortar estate of the campus. The large scale and the glossy renderings of master plan projects such as Cornell Tech and Manhattanville mean that in the world of university planning, it is the vast new campuses and campus extensions that draw the attention and excitement. Nonetheless, opportunities like these are infrequent and rarely the most feasible means of addressing higher education's evolving challenges. More often than not, the physical environment of a university is shaped by what we are calling the 'revitalizing' master plan, by which is meant a planning exercise of any scale aimed at augmenting and breathing new life into hitherto overlooked, underperforming areas of the university estate.

Higher education institutions of all sizes, types, and academic standards are contemplating future growth by looking within their existing land holdings and campus systems, and developing formal strategies to ensure its districts function to maximum efficiency with the ultimate goal of creating an attractive, sustainable environment that can support the academic needs of its users over the long term. This is not a new trend, but is one that is gathering in momentum and sophistication as urban, suburban, and greenfield universities strive to deliver vibrant, thriving places of learning and living against a background of pinched budgets, finite land reserves, and an ageing building stock.

New master plans of this kind typically involve a series of general steps: first, the analysis of the existing physical environment; second, the determining of institutional principles and objectives; next, identifying opportunities for refurbishment and infill construction, such as existing surface car parks; lastly, formulating campus framework systems and related implementation strategies, both short and long term. The principles addressed within this master-plan type fall predominantly within three overlapping categories: supporting institutional mission; stimulating cross-campus connections; and enhancing the public realm. Customarily the scope of such plans extends some 10 or more years into the future, enabling institutions to plan for long-range growth to create a coherent yet pliant campus.

In the large majority of cases, the initial impetus behind revitalizing master plans is a simple but pressing demand: the need for more floor space. More residences, more places to socialize and study informally, bigger and better flexible laboratories amongst other facilities are required to satisfy the requirements and expectations of the growing university community. Particularly for space-squeezed urban and suburban institutions, revitalizing master plans can be a valuable tool in getting more capacity of their existing estate. This was the driving force behind the University of Oxford's decision to commission a master planning exercise for their South Parks Science Area (master plan endorsed by the city council in 2013). The uncoordinated, piecemeal growth of the precinct over the past 150 years has resulted in an exceptionally dense concentration of buildings, confusing to navigate, impenetrable, and built tightly to the boundaries of its city-centre site. For many years, it has not met the university's functional, aesthetic, and environmental standards. To retain its leading position at the forefront of research and development, however, the university faces an acute pressure to ensure that the calibre of its science facilities remains amongst the best in the world. The South Parks Science Area master plan provides a strategic vision for its coherent growth over the next 20 years. Most fundamentally, it delivers a framework to increase the Area's floor plan by as much as 50 per cent by a combined programme of refurbishment, the removal of existing buildings that are not fit for purpose, and new construction that will answer to the university's long-term needs. In the second instance, it seeks to make the precinct a more welcoming, attractive, and user-friendly space through infrastructure and landscape interventions. It proposes a new east–west pedestrian spine to enhance legibility and linkages; a coordinated landscape structure of trees and public realm; and the rationalization of servicing arrangements. The plan is a vehicle to enable the maximization of the site by first considering it as a holistic entity, and then parcelling it into a series of discrete development projects, each consisting of notional building envelopes and their surrounding public realm.

Science precincts are common targets of revitalizing master plans. The challenge to keep apace with the technological progress often gives rise to incremental construction patterns and thus to chaotic and confusing layouts. In continental Europe, the mid-twentieth century trend for universities to relocate their science facilities from city centres to satellite campuses resulted frequently in low-density, piecemeal sites, characterized by bland architecture and atmospheres of lifelessness and isolation, especially outside of working hours.

The University of Oxford's Science Area master plan outlines a route to create additional floor space within a dense, unstructured city-centre site.

Several institutions have taken steps to improve these campuses through remedial master plans. In the Netherlands, for example, Utrecht University commissioned OMA in 1988 to devise a master plan for its De Uithof satellite site that would transform it from a desolate commuter campus to a community more akin to an Anglo-American model. The master plan proposed a concentration of buildings of varying functions to cure the low-density Uithof from its 'addiction to space'. Since implementation, the campus has begun to evolve into a breeding ground of experimental architecture laid out in a dense, Kasbah-like framework. Similarly, ETH Zürich has implemented an innovative plan to transform its secluded, 32-hectare (80-acre) Hönggerberg satellite campus into a Science City (see pages 202–5). The plan aimed to reshape the monofunctional compound into an urban community through infill development which doubled the floor space, diversified the land use by adding residences and social facilities, and provided opportunities for collaborative research. The master plan is central to ETH's institutional goals, for it is anticipated that the revitalized Science City will attract scientific talent from around the world.

The Oxford Science Area or ETH Zürich Science City master plans were formulated to target a specific section of the institutional estate. Revitalizing master plans can, moreover, be applied to address the whole of a university's land holdings. This was the case with the 2020 Estates Vision (2012) of the UK's University of Hertfordshire. Through its application, the university is aiming to ameliorate its user-unfriendly

environment by creating new special places within its public realm. An underutilized green space is scheduled to be transformed into a vibrant outdoor events plaza with clear links to the university's social venue, Club de Havilland.

Hertfordshire is characteristic of the campus typology to which revitalizing master plans have often been applied: the post-war campus, originally built to a rigid layout that is now struggling to address large surges in student numbers unforeseen at the time of its design. Around the world, the post-war era brought an unprecedented growth in the higher education system. Large numbers of new, whole-cloth campuses were constructed, characterized by a bold spirit of Modernist experimentation. While their cutting-edge architecture and strong layouts appeared in the 1950s and 1960s as an embodiment of this age of possibility, progress, and openness, by the twenty-first century many administrators are finding that they no longer satisfy all the demands of modern-day education. In many respects, the universities that have grown organically over many decades or centuries present much less of a challenge to those charged with managing their estates than the post-war whole-cloth campus. The visionary layouts of the latter were, generally speaking, conceived to answer to the requirements of the day and planned as an entity to a strong but inherently unyielding design vision.

At many HEIs, the pressure to accommodate bigger student populations and different types of facilities in the intervening years has resulted in unstructured physical growth that, because of the inflexibility of the original template, has compromised the physical experience of the campus. When carefully conceived and deftly applied, revitalizing master plans can remedy these situations by providing a forward-looking strategy for meeting long-term functional requirements while creating the type of welcoming, aesthetically-pleasing spatial experience that attracts the best staff and students. As many post-war universities reach their semicentennial or more, this approach is becoming increasingly more valuable and more prevalent.

The University of Lancaster in Britain had found itself in this situation when, in 2006, it commissioned John McAslan and Partners to produce a master plan to reconsolidate its estate. Lancaster belongs to the 1960s generation of UK New Universities, built in scenic greenfield locations by some of the country's leading architects. Decades of rogue building had broken the plan's original rigid geometry, impeded way-finding, and left the once-vibrant social core bleak and lifeless. McAslan's ten-year master plan (2007, reassessed in 2012) established a directional strategy to reinvigorate the campus by addressing social spaces and pedestrian routes through the central spine. Its on-going implementation has resulted in infill construction, renovations, and major landscaping schemes, such as George Fox Square, to enhance the campus setting. Above all, commented *Building Design*,

> The masterplan has been about place-making and investing in the public realm. 'Our success at Lancaster is that so far we have managed to convince the university that they need to spread the investment into the spaces between the buildings – the social and physical infrastructure,' says [McAslan director Aidan] Potter. 'The triumph is that they've seen they have to invest in the public realm.'[45]

The public realm is a key ingredient in creating the sense of place that is uniquely associated with the campus experience. Encompassing roads, pavements, parks, plazas, and all other open spaces that comprise the arteries and focal points of the campus framework, the public realm is the locus where interaction occurs. Making these spaces attractive, welcoming, and memorable enriches the ways in which university life is experienced and thus their improvement is a regular concern of revitalizing master plans. In 2012, Curtin University in Australia launched its Place Activation Plan, a key objective of which was to address failings in its public realm and thereby boost its place-centric identity.[46] Again, Curtin is a post-war institution.

The plan divides the 116-hectare (285-acre) campus in Perth, dominated by austere Brutalist and Postmodern buildings, into a series of precincts, one of which is identified as the central spine that runs the north–south length of the campus. The plan renames this promenade the Curtin Corso, and reimagines it as a 'lineal meeting plaza' populated by comfortable seating, shade, shelter, visual interest, and sub-destinations such as food carts. With a limited range of cultural, leisure, and dining facilities to engage students after lectures end, the Perth campus currently becomes a ghost town once the sun sets. Interventions such as the Corso are intended to create the meaningful places that it currently lacks, places where all members of the university community want to spend time.

The creation of welcoming spaces would contribute little, however, if they were not well connected within the campus network. Successful connections between the different parts of campus are critical to establishing a continuous fabric. Curtin suffers from longstanding problems of poor way-finding and incoherent circulatory routes. The sprawling, disparate site contributed greatly to the lack of cohesion. Whether pedestrian, vehicular, or cyclist, connections serve as the physical and social links on campus, as sites of circulation but also of community interaction. Under the Place Activation Plan, the regenerated Curtin Corso is projected to fulfil these dual objectives. Immediate, short-term actions such as removing barriers, free-standing signage, and elements that inhibit movement and sightlines are intended to ease circulation and enhance vistas that connect key destinations in a way that improves navigation. Way-finding is projected to become an intuitive process, through a themed combination of landmarks, landscape treatments, and signage. Moreover, by transforming the promenade into a lineal plaza through streetscape and landscape improvements, journeying across the campus will become a pleasurable experience. As Aidan Potter reflected of Lancaster, 'It is important to pay attention to brand and place-management issues. Masterplanning [sic] has to grow up and become comfortable with these words.'[47]

Physical change can be a potent means of stimulating change in many directions. Carefully conceived and deftly applied, master plans can revitalize campus holdings to deliver this change, employing creative means to ensure that existing facilities are used to the maximum.

Opposite: Curtin University's new pedestrian spine as envisaged in the Place Activation Plan. It proposes extra seating, shade, food stalls, and bicycle storage.

Student Accomodation

Lighting

Open Flexible Street

Remove Central 'Cyclone'

Bike Pods

Alfresco Seating

Eat Street

Market Space

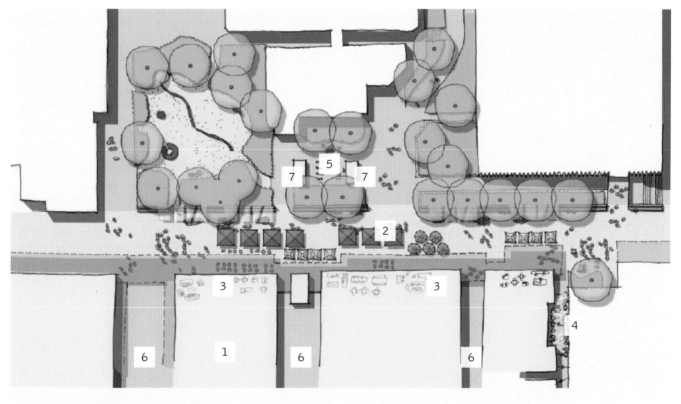

1. North Village
2. Market Stalls
3. Eat Street
4. Activate Laneways
5. Bike Storage, Seating and Shade Elements
6. Strong East–West Links through North Village
7. Bike Pods

ONLINE LEARNING

From banking to retail, newspapers to socializing, online technology is changing all aspects of our lives. Higher education, too, is being swept headlong into the digital revolution. In a study concerning the physical or tangible realm of universities – their architecture and master planning – it may well appear incongruous to introduce the very intangible subject of online learning. Yet the extent of its ramifications upon the delivery of tertiary education is such that it would be ill-considered not to briefly consider its ambit and future, particularly to surmise any future effects upon the nature of campus design.

Within the online learning phenomenon, the buzzword of the moment is MOOC. The MOOC – the acronym for massive open online course – emerged in 2011. At first, its purview was limited to specialist higher education press and blogs, but in 2012 the phenomenon entered the mainstream. That year, one of the three major MOOC providers, Coursera, signed up 33 leading universities to provide more than 200 online courses to 2.2 million users, all for free.[48]

MOOCs are a new educational model fusing teaching and social networking. They are free, open-access, scalable online courses of higher education level, developed independently by academics or through a contractual partnership between a university and third party platform. The evolving concept employs various online resources, such as videos and message boards, in place of traditional practices of academic learning. Universities have long published lectures online. An initiative of online lectures and course material under the umbrella title OpenCourseWare, for example, began in 1999 when the University of Tübingen began publishing some lectures online. Similar projects followed in the US at MIT, Yale, University of Michigan, and University of California Berkeley. Yet MOOCs represent an evolution. This is the first time that free, full-course programmes are offered designed specifically for digital consumption. The key breakthrough is the integration of academic lectures, which can be watched and re-watched at the students own pace, with interactive coursework, classmate evaluation, and automated tests. Other fee-based functions are being developed, such as career services. They are, moreover, as their title suggests, massive in scale. Unlimited numbers of students can potentially enrol onto the courses.[49] Working on such a scale inevitably means that students have no individual contact with the faculty leading the courses.

The model is still in development stages. It was only in 2011 that Stanford professor Sebastian Thrun with computer scientist Peter Norvig created an online version of their artificial intelligence class which attracted 160,000 subscribers in 209 countries. From this experiment, the MOOC movement was born.[50] Thrun went on to found Udacity, one of the three major MOOC platforms alongside Coursera (a for-profit start-up launched by two Stanford computer scientists) and edX (a non-profit partnership set up by MIT and Harvard which has expanded to include 14 institutions).[51] It is overwhelmingly American-driven, but the phenomenon is spreading. Coursera, for example, has enlisted over 20 international institutions, including the National University of Singapore and the University of Copenhagen, as content providers. Udacity students have staged 'meet-ups' in nearly 450 cities across the globe. Britain entered the market late in 2012 when the distance-learning organization, Open University, announced the launch of FutureLearn Ltd., offering free, online courses from an initial consortium of 11 universities, including the University of Exeter and the University of Bristol. 2013 saw the inauguration of a pan-European MOOC initiative, OpenUpEd, drawing together partners in 11 countries, including France, the Netherlands, Slovakia and Turkey, and beginning with some 40 courses. The same year, China moved into the field with the launch of XuetangX by C9-league Tsinghua University, a platform hosting local MOOCs from some of China's most prestigious institutions.

The rationale behind this digital revolution is clear. Demands for a university education are soaring across the world at the same time as it is becoming more expensive to attain one. In the past two decades, tuition and fees at standard non-profit US colleges have grown from averages of $17,000 to $29,000, while the colleges themselves now carry 88 per cent more debt than in 2001 as more and more capital has been invested in new facilities to justify the fees.[52] MOOCs have the potential to broaden the outreach of higher education to those who would otherwise find it unaffordable. The total number of students from Lithuania who registered for Udacity's first course outstripped the entire student population of Stanford.[53] Millions of people, whoever they are and wherever they live, can share the extensive knowledge of distinguished academics. In turn, universities can engage with new and potential students on a scale never before anticipated. MOOCs have been billed as offering a 'try before you buy' function, enabling prospective students to make more informed decisions upon their subject and institution choices. Yet they are also heralded as a boon for those post-university age, supplying career-long learning in accessible, cost-effective formats.

Champions advocate that online learning could even yield benefits to the onsite university experience. When Harvard and MIT publicized a combined investment of $60 million into edX in 2013, they justified the move by emphasizing that they saw the platform as a vehicle to test new teaching methods that could then be appropriated on their campuses. The centuries-old lecture model needs updating, so argued Sanjay Sarma, MIT's director of digital learning. Online instruction carries the potential of releasing lesson time for more innovative and interactive activities.[54]

Notwithstanding these attractions, MOOCs elicit fervent debate. Is the template of free education financially sustainable in the long term? Will universities lose control of their products if they partner with a commercial platform? Can the courses be accredited in a manner that will satisfy employer requirements? Can an online-only education invest students with the skills and the social experience of a traditional university education? Coursera's co-founder, Andrew Ng, has drawn attention to the latter. 'We make some of our best friends in college,' he has said, gaining social skills for which video and text-chat cannot compensate.[55] Reservations have been raised, moreover, about the pedagogical quality of MOOCs due to their scale, largely predicated upon the lack of personalized feedback. Their record of drop-outs is also extremely high. Sixty thousand enrolled in Duke University's Introduction to Astronomy on Coursera in 2012, only for 96.5 per cent to withdraw before the end.

MOOC providers must convince students and employers alike that they provide the learning and qualifications to which they aspire. A pressing issue is accreditation. While different means of recognizing MOOCs for academic credit are being explored, currently very few courses have any form of accreditation. In 2013, Coursera introduced a 'signature track' that gives students a more meaningful certification of their efforts in exchange for a fee. Late the same year, Thrun announced Udacity's move away from the academic course template towards practical, industry-specific courses which would charge fees for assistance and certification of completion. Such services are likely to play a material role in developing online platforms into sustainable business models in the future.[56]

It is too early to predict the outcome that MOOCs will have on the long-term provision of higher education, or how individual universities will have to adapt. The online learning tableau is advancing on a month-by-month basis. The current zeal may be the result of aggressive marketing and the enthusiasm that innovation naturally engenders. As it currently stands, the template is tangential to the core work of higher education organizations.[57]

Nonetheless, what MOOCs represent is a fundamental reshaping of the relationship between scholars, students and institutions. Any decisive global move to this approach would bring considerable change and, inevitably, much uncertainty to the university realm. Thrun forecast in 2012 that within 50 years, only 10 universities will remain in the world. And Thrun is not alone in this view.[58] A stream of articles has prophesized that in only decades from now the traditional university campus as we know it will be rendered defunct by a digital utopia; 'clicks and mortar' will replace bricks and mortar. Yet just as 1990s predictions that teleworking would prove the demise of the central business district were not fulfilled, such auguries for the university campus should not be accepted as inevitable.

The precedents of other sectors suggest that online delivery operations can develop alongside traditional approaches before behavioural patterns radically alter.[59] The magic of university life is about far more than information delivery, and the physical environment of an HEI delivers a breadth of community services that virtual domains cannot replicate. Experiential learning cannot be replaced, campuses will not become extinct, and universities will not stop building. MOOCs are just one aspect of a digital movement that is causing waves in the traditional teaching, learning, research, and interaction patterns of higher education. The sustained adoption and refinement of this movement is, nevertheless, likely to have implications on the campus estate both in the building typology of new construction and in an (even more) increased emphasis on the student experience.

Traditional lecture theatres are already becoming less important on campus, and the pedagogical evolution of which MOOCs are a part is likely to intensify this trend. An increasing emphasis on online lecture delivery may mean that future building projects are dominated by laboratory construction and interstitial or 'hub' spaces, rather than conventional classrooms. Ultimately, their presence gives more impetus to the importance of designing inherently flexible structures that are able to accommodate future priorities. Furthermore, as online models become more sophisticated and build reputations, administrators will be faced with the challenge of convincing future students to choose an orthodox – and costly – place-based university degree instead of a MOOC-based education. The physical environment of a campus will be a cogent weapon in their arsenal.

Whether MOOCs will justify the current fervour over the long-term is still in debate. Nonetheless, they may come to hold a valuable place in the university landscape, and institutions must consider how to respond to them carefully and proactively.

LOOKING TO THE FUTURE

Notwithstanding Sebastian Thrun's death-knell predictions for the destiny of the place-based university, the objective of this section is to examine what the near-future holds for the planning and architecture of the physical campus. What factors are likely to shape its evolution? Which building and master-plan typologies are poised to grow in importance?

Broadly speaking, running through the 'trends' outlined in the preceding pages are three underpinning leitmotifs: place, access, and efficiency. Place: this encompasses the urgency to deliver the calibre of faculty and student experience that elevates an institution above the crowded field of competitors, both by answering to their social and learning needs and by investing a campus with the type of attractive, welcoming landscapes and buildings that elicit topophilia. Access: this refers to expanding access to higher education, through enlarging the footprint of existing HEIs and thereby raising capacity and through the establishment of new institutions, both standalone, satellite, and partnership campuses. Efficiency: by which is meant ensuring that a university's physical estate is designed to operate efficiently now and in forthcoming decades. It encompasses the need to identify and accommodate long-range academic and strategic goals that will enable an HEI to maintain its relevance. Flexibility of space is critical to this. These are the themes which are currently conditioning the approach to architecture and planning and which are set to continue doing so in coming decades.

Place
Online learning has the potential to revolutionize the international higher education industry like nothing else before. Yet it is improbable that cyber education will ever displace place-based institutions. When we think of a university experience, so many of the ideas that are invoked are linked to physical space. As a setting for formal interaction – in classrooms, laboratories, offices – and informal gatherings – on lawns, in cafeterias, residence halls – the campus is an emotional, visceral, and social space. It is integral to the mental picture built by prospective students as they make their application choices, and is the backdrop embedded in the memories of alumni and faculty. Buildings and landscapes are long-term assets. On a pragmatic level, they provide indispensable access to research equipment and other resources. From a psychological perspective, they create an arena for the social interaction which is fundamental to a rounded education. A lasting commitment to the built environment, from the arcades of the University of Virginia's Lawn (begun 1817) to the UK New Universities of the 1960s, has created a cornerstone for attracting high-quality students and faculty. The role of the built environment in the university experience is deep-rooted and, for much of the higher education industry, this will not diminish in the future.

But to survive and, moreover, to thrive, the physical environments of HEIs must adapt. The nexus of challenges now facing the tertiary education system – rising operational costs, diminishing public funding, mounting competition at home and abroad, the rapid advance of technology and theories of learning – will intensify as the twenty-first century rolls on. Notwithstanding the deep-rooted and ongoing relevance of the university as a physical entity, even the world's most prestigious institutions cannot rest on their laurels.

Progressively over time, the cost of an on-site university education will become comparatively more expensive for the student. The student who selects this degree path over an online or distance-learning alternative will, therefore, expect more from their learning experience. The campus environment will gain in importance. The enduring university will maximize the value of 'place' to a more considered, integrated, and sustainable degree than ever before. To rise to the summons posed by virtual learning and international competition, HEIs must give added importance to the effective use of their physical environments to create destinations that enhance the educational experience.

It is hard to imagine otherwise than that the eye-catching, gravity-defying, headline-making buildings of Libeskind, Gehry, and others will continue to appeal to university administrators and donors in the quest for architecturally exciting destinations. Of the single-building trends profiled in these pages, though, it is that of hub buildings that has the potential to bring the most immediate advantages to the student experience. Creating a forum for dialogue supported by wireless connectivity, interactive displays, AV equipment and more, extant examples such as the Exeter Forum or Coventry Hub have set an example for how this building type can promote the new dynamics of student learning whilst simultaneously providing a geographical and psychological focus for the university community. The hub concept is likely to evolve, taking on more functions as the realm of the 'third place' becomes more important to campus life alongside the growth of virtual learning. By providing a consolidation of services – retail, dining, administration, study – within a super-networked space, this building type will reflect the new 'blended', immersive academic experience while bringing different user-groups together. The blurring of boundaries that is already happening in instances such as the Coventry Hub will continue as distinctions between learning and social spaces, formal and informal interaction, become more and more fluid.

Fluidity will also increasingly be applied to describe the interaction of campus and city. The link between city and campus is a topic of rich discussion at the moment. As demonstrated by the language of urbanism that projects such as Columbia's Manhattanville and North West Cambridge engage to define their goals, the idea of the city is an important impetus for the built and programmatic form of campuses. This is likely to intensify in the future.

As one commentator has observed, 'both students and recent graduates – for many of whom university campuses are the de facto training ground in urban life – seem to want to be in places that have the busy vibrancy and easy amenities of both campus and town centre'.[60] The type of commercial development personified by Storrs Center or Discovery Rise that mixes academic facilities with residential, retail, and community services upon an urban model will feature progressively within estate investments. It is likely that the model – now dominated overwhelmingly by North American examples – will become a more common feature in other developed and developing higher education systems around the world as HEIs set about maximizing their business performance and gaining the edge over competitors. As it does so, the template will itself evolve. Further opportunities will be refined and made place-specific, such as that of university-linked retirement communities, all with the goal of enabling institutions to capitalize on their resources and expertise.

Access
This is the most straightforward of the themes in nature, if not in delivery. To answer the forecasts for the surge in graduate numbers, the current capacity of the higher education industry will have to increase. Notwithstanding the potential for online learning to accommodate some of this growth, large-scale expansion and new institutions,

particularly outside the old West, are inevitable. The burgeoning appetite for higher education beyond its traditional Western confines will impel and be assuaged by the founding of new independent institutions and by transnational experiments.

The latter's future longevity is hard to predict. They bring the benefit of established institutional reputation and experience, but do not necessarily carry the same degree of permanence. Many of the international branch campus ventures hitherto trialed have been tentative ones, housed in leased premises; many have failed. Generally speaking, successful universities tend to have extremely long-sighted views on their physical assets. As mentioned earlier, more than 70 per cent of international branch campuses are not fully-owned by their parent institution.[61] This statistic does raise concerns about the resilience of the model over the long term. When it comes to transnational enterprises, it is those 30 per cent of institutions that invest in the built infrastructure which suggest a deep-vested, long-range involvement in augmenting the educational provision of that nation; these are the endeavours that are likely to have a lasting future.

Efficiency
Planning, designing, and building for the long-term will be ever more important to the future of a successful HEI. The space requirements of an HEI have multiplied far more rapidly than commercial or residential sectors for instance, and many estates now include superannuated and underused properties and landscapes. This inefficiency undermines a university's financial and environmental sustainability. As we look into the future, comprehensive, long-range master planning will, more than ever, be needed to ensure that facilities answer long-term goals through flexibility and appropriate scale. The time-tested practice of revitalizing master plans will be increasingly valuable as a critical tool in the stewardship of the campus. By assessing the existing building stock, and identifying opportunities for infill development, landscape improvements, and adaptive reuse of outdated properties, they can help maximize the best value out of a campus, and ensure it supports institutional objectives through physical quality and identity.

Flexibility will be an essential quality inherent within the next era of revitalizing master plans. It will, of course, be equally important in the case of new campus planning and large-scale expansions. To ensure that campuses remain

valued and viable long into the future, their master plan must prioritize flexibility. This focus is the best guarantee of safeguarding against the vagaries of fashion and pace of technology. Fashions and technologies will change, and architecture in particular must not be too submissive to them as design parameters. To design to a particular technology or to a single department will result in early obsolescence; to future-proof as much as possible against evolving technology, teaching methodologies, and research priorities, the very essence of any design must be the ability to adapt. New spaces need to be conceived with versatility of use in mind. Nowhere is this case clearer than in the present generation of interdisciplinary science research buildings.

Interdisciplinary research buildings are, and will continue to be, one of the biggest foci of institutional investment. They encapsulate two of the greatest drivers for change on campus: interdisciplinary dialogue and the STEM subjects. The mounting prominence attached to these core disciplines will not abate, especially within emerging economies, and will be reflected in a growing number of buildings commissioned to foster translational study and work. Interdisciplinary centres such as MIT's long-established Media Lab already demonstrate a growing tide towards a curriculum of applied education, fuelled largely by postgraduate student demand.[62] The development of the Cornell Tech campus is a case in point. Boasting an unusual cross disciplinary emphasis, Cornell's provost has explained that instead of 'creating the traditional academic structure of faculties, schools, or departments,' it is 'creating focus areas or hubs'.[63] These will concentrate on connective media, healthier life, and the built environment, but the master plan calls for the hubs to evolve to address emerging industries in forthcoming years.

Cornell Tech is a vivid example of how orthodox priorities are evolving to ensure the university maintains its bearing to a rapidly evolving society. The impetus for cross-collaboration and the blurring of academic boundaries will be met by a rising tide of another of our 'trends' – joint-venture buildings. In both practical and conceptual terms, this building type is likely to be increasingly valuable. From a pragmatic perspective, the cost-sharing benefits are clear; particularly when applied to advanced scientific study, joint-venture schemes will facilitate the pooling of resources

without which the same depth of research would not be financially feasible. On an ideological level, by establishing partnerships will their peers, with public research bodies, and with industry, universities are opening the doors to fertile collaborations that can bolster academic output, promote entrepreneurialism, and generate industry revenue. Partnerships for the shared use of buildings will encompass cultural and recreational facilities, enterprise-driven incubators and business parks, and research laboratories. University-industry partnerships will be a principal driver, resulting in more building projects on and off campus, such as the ETH Zürich-IBM Binning and Rohrer Nanotechnology Centre (2011), as universities push to maintain their relevance both financially and in the quality of research output within science and innovation.

For hundreds of years, planning a campus had a generally stable formula, based on place requirements for teaching, dining, sleeping, and entertainment. Now, higher education is facing an unprecedented pace of change which is having significant effects upon the approach to campus development. For many decades, campus design was a matter of commissioning a master planner to produce a site layout to guide construction. Today, the scenario is much more complex. Universities comprise some of the biggest and most complex physical environments in the world. The need to deliver flexible, immersive places to learn, the advent of transnational education, and the scope of commercial or joint-venture enterprises necessitates that a university's physical assets are part of a clear development strategy. Campus design is not an isolated action, but should be thought of in terms of a sequential activity to be undertaken once the institutional strategic aims have been determined. The importance of thorough and careful forethought cannot be emphasized enough. To strengthen their power of 'place', to answer to the burgeoning enrolment figures, and to ensure they flexibly meet space and strategic needs in the future, campuses require a sensitive development framework that addresses place-making, assets, efficiency, and commercialization. The long-term durability of a place-based university is contingent upon the whole of its physical estate operating in concert to achieve these goals. The task is not an easy one, it will necessitate increasingly sophisticated planning approaches; but when properly realized it will safeguard the rich tradition of campus design and ensure that higher education's legacy of place is perpetuated throughout the twenty-first century and beyond.

Opposite: Campus expansion plans, such as that for the Universidad del Istmo in Guatemala, will increase the current capacity of global higher education.

TWO.ONE

ADAPTIVE REUSE

NEW CAMPUS
CENTRAL SAINT MARTINS

London, UK 2011 £145m 40,000m² (430,000ft²)
Architect: Stanton Williams

JUST BEHIND KING'S CROSS STATION – ONE OF LONDON'S GREAT
VICTORIAN RAILWAY TERMINI – LIES THE SITE OF ONE OF
EUROPE'S LARGEST REGENERATION PROJECTS.

ROBUST BRICK SOUTH FACADE Here
emblazoned with with a temporary art
installation, part of a serial public art
programme in King's Cross.

Early in 2006, planning permission was granted to transform 27 hectares (67 acres) of derelict railway lands and warehouses – hitherto a nocturnal backdrop for many unsavoury aspects of city life – into a vibrant quarter known as King's Cross Central boasting a full complement of retail, offices, dining, and performance spaces. At the physical and ideological heart of this scheme sits the new campus of Central Saint Martins, part of the University of the Arts London.

Although one of the world's most highly-regarded art and design colleges since its creation in 1989,[1] Central Saint Martins did not have a physical estate to match. Early in the twenty-first century, the college resolved to consolidate the jumble of buildings spread across central London which housed its activities and it embarked upon a spirited decision to relocate wholesale to become part of King's Cross Central.

The development offered a unique opportunity: a large site within a future creative and cultural hub, with first-rate national and international transport links. It also offered the college's architects, Stanton Williams, a rousing challenge. Rather than take up residence in one of the quarter's

approximately 50 planned new buildings, the institution instead opted for a bold, part-adaptive reuse scheme focusing on an 1852 Granary Building, an imposing six-storey survivor of the area's industrial past.[2] Its burly 50-metre (165-foot) long brick elevation was reimagined as the public face of the art school's campus and the focal point of a new communal square.

Opened in 2011, the scheme was designed specifically to encourage collaborations between departments. Containing 40,000 square metres (430,500 square feet) over four levels of multi-purpose workshops and specialist studios, this is a building on a truly urban scale. The soaring warehouse dimensions of the Granary Building are used to dramatic effect as a cavernous, public-accessible lobby, with a library housed on its upper floors. Bookstacks are arranged between original iron columns and timber joists, while thick-set numerals identify what were once grain chutes and now function as windows.[3] Two contemporaneous transit sheds running parallel to the north of the Granary were adapted to house studios, shops, and bars.[4] The historic horse stables below the eastern shed were converted to form cycle stores.

The transit sheds flank a large new insertion to the site, centred upon a vast indoor 'street'. Stretching 110 metres (360 feet) and crossed by bridges and stairs, this central axis was envisaged as the nucleus of college activity where the institutional ambitions of collaboration and interaction could thrive. Teaching accommodation is ranged in two volumes either side. Glazed walls create a framework of flexible, transparent spaces that invite interactions and interdisciplinarity. Although similar in scale and massing to its industrial neighbours, the new-build addition quietly distinguishes itself through a contemporary union of translucent roof, glass partitions, and raw concrete surfaces.

As a whole, the architecture of the scheme is characterized by large, well-lit spaces, and a palette of simple, sturdy materials. The material finishes are often modest in their range – notably concrete slabs and plywood walls – evidencing the straitened economic climate during which construction took place. Yet this

VAST ENTRY LOBBY The lobby opens towards the internal 'street'. Turnstiles divide the publicly-accessible narthex from the inner academic realm.

GROUND FLOOR PLAN Accommodation consists of the restored Granary Building and Transit Sheds, plus a vast modern addition of central street flanked by four storeys of teaching studios.

notwithstanding, the fusion of old and new has been handled gracefully and impressively. The patina of the grain store and transit sheds thoughtfully reveals their industrial pasts, while the new additions provide a blank canvas onto which the life of the college will imprint itself as its staff and students take root. 'Plato's grove, the idea of the park, the cloister, the arcade and enfilade — they are all here,' appraised *Building Design*. 'This is a real gathering place, a vast, warm, horizontal version of Oskar Schlemmer's populated Bauhaus staircase picture. You can learn here, and you will remember it.'[5]

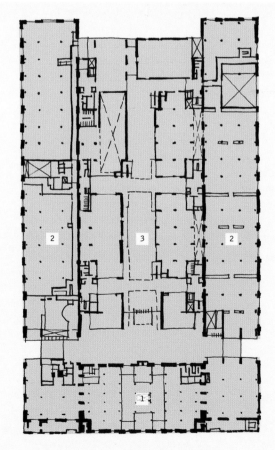

1. Granary Building
2. Transit Sheds
3. Central Street

SIX-STOREY GRANARY BUILDING
Once a grain storehouse at the height of London's industrial boom, it now houses a library and offices. It faces a new public square, one of the city's largest.

FEDERAL BUILDING
KENDALL COLLEGE OF ART AND DESIGN

Michigan, USA 2012 $23m 8,500m² (91,000ft²)
Architect: TowerPinkster

THE FEDERAL BUILDING STARTED LIFE IN 1909 AS A POST
OFFICE AND COURTHOUSE, A CLASSICAL BEAUX ARTS PRESENCE
OCCUPYING AN ENTIRE BLOCK AT THE HEART OF THE MICHIGAN
CITY OF GRAND RAPIDS.

CREATIVELY REPURPOSED Entries no longer in use have been enterprisingly adapted into study and gathering spaces. The original plaster and woodwork have been painstakingly restored.

Designed by James Knox Taylor, supervising architect for the US Treasury, its significance was recognized in 1974 with the inclusion on the National Register of Historic Places. By 2008, this once formidable granite landmark was, though, sadly neglected. Vacant and deteriorating, it required a daunting itinerary of repairs. It was at this point that in stepped Kendall college of Art and Design and Ferris State University. Since the art college had become affiliated with Ferris State in 2001, its student numbers had soared from 520 to 1,400 eventuating in a serious space shortage. The Federal Building, sitting directly opposite to Kendall's extent properties, was ideally positioned to answer its calls for additional facilities.

In 2010, construction work began to recast its aging fabric into an education building housing an auditorium, library, galleries, café, workshops, classrooms, and communal space. The transformation presented challenges on several levels, not least its financing. Funds were raised via a public-private partnership which drew upon a range of city, county, state, and federal resources, capturing tax credits available for historic preservation projects. Such a multi-level partnership inevitably required an integrated collaboration amongst the various agencies involved, which, because of the building's listed status, also included the National Parks Service and Michigan Historic Preservation Office.

The improvements required to the structural envelope, interior, and infrastructure were considerable. The roof leaked extensively, the solid granite veneer was crumbling; inside, rooms were water-damaged; mechanical, electrical, and plumbing infrastructures were wholly outdated. Nonetheless, notwithstanding tight budgetary constraints, a key goal of the project was to preserve as much of Taylor's fabric as possible to maintain the historic integrity of the local landmark. The façade was tuck pointed and cleaned, the wooden windows were restored with energy-efficient glazing added, the interior oak panelling was revived, and the marble, terrazzo, and mosaic floors were repaired. In total, 95 per cent of existing walls and floors and over 200 doors and light fittings were reused.

Yet this emphasis upon perpetuating the architectural identity of a building originally configured to house federal courts and post office had to be countermanded against the programmatic requirements of a modern art school. Restoring the building would have been futile if it was not fit for purpose. Its listed status did complicate the task. Razing internal walls was often prohibited, but selected walls were allowed to be removed to enlarge spaces, and thereby answer Kendall's needs for spacious collaborative design classrooms and studios. Once-covered skylights were reinstated to bring natural light to an exhibitions area. Every inch of the building was reinterpreted to answer its new function. Thus its marble-floored hallways have become student common areas, furnished with sofas, tables, and chairs for informal study and socializing. Redundant revolving door entryways have been imaginatively recast as study niches.

The ethos of the project was to safeguard architectural identity while creating a functional learning and teaching resource. In parts, the building looks exactly as it would have done in the 1910s; in others, courtrooms and congressional offices have been transformed into lecture halls and computer suites equipped with the latest educational technology. In the Federal Building, the aesthetic and the practical have been carefully balanced.

FROM CORRIDOR TO COMMON AREA Almost every inch of the building has been repurposed to meet Kendal's needs. Corridors are now venues for socializing and studying.

FROM COURTROOM TO LECTURE HALL Architectural elements and details were preserved throughout.

FROM COURTHOUSE TO COLLEGE In its hundred-year history this Beaux-Arts building has evolved and adapted to meet the changing needs of its local community.

THE BOILERHOUSE
UNIVERSITY OF WESTERN SYDNEY

Sydney, Australia 2011 Aus$4m
Architect: Tanner Kibble Denton Architects

THE PARRAMATTA CAMPUS OF THE UNIVERSITY OF
WESTERN SYDNEY (UWS) IS AN EXAMPLE OF ADAPTIVE
REUSE WRIT LARGE.

BUILT IN 1894 as a laundry and heating facility,
the Boilerhouse stood crumbling, unused and
unloved, until a 2009–11 project saw it transformed
into the heart of a new student precinct.

Since 1813, it has functioned as a school for orphans, the Rydalmere Hospital for the Insane, and, from 1998, as one of UWS's six campuses. This case study focuses on the site's most recent reuse project, the conversion of an 1894 boiler house into a dining and social space.

By 2009, the campus was thriving. Its population had leaped from 5,000 to 9,000 in just two years, and further growth was forecast. However, its public domain left much to be desired. The incremental development of the site as a whole had left a series of underutilized spaces, most notably a lifeless central plaza. The campus lacked a 'third place', somewhere that acted as a focal point for informal gathering. Given the anticipated increase in student numbers, the need to create social spaces and student facilities became pressing, and this led to the planning of a new student precinct at the physical heart of the campus. Tanner Kibble Denton Architects designed a new pedestrian concourse that connected the main anchors of university life – the library and lecture theatres – and encouraged interaction and vitality by providing welcoming places to linger, eat, and unwind. The cornerstone of the scheme was the Boilerhouse.

Originally built as an industrial laundry and heating facility for the Rydalmere Hospital, the Boilerhouse's tall brick chimney was a landmark on campus. Since a fire in 1996, however, it had stood derelict. Located at the centre of campus, it occupied an ideal position for a student hub, whilst also presenting an opportunity to uphold and celebrate the special heritage of the site. The devised scheme was a sympathetic and responsive conversion that preserved as much of the original character of the structure as practicable in order to invest the new public precinct with a unique identity.

The existing wooden rafters and trusses, brickwork, and remains of the original timber sarking were retained, and a new lantern roof was added. Gauges, auto-stokers, ducts, and steam valves were conserved, while the historic boilers served as the centrepiece of a playful public art programme and now sit, sandblasted and refashioned, on plinths in front of the building. A commerical kitchen was inserted, linking the Boilerhouse to the major new element of the scheme – an open-air pavilion. Housing additional dining and seating options, the pavilion echoed the form of its nineteenth-century neighbour with an extruded stylization of its roofline. However, its choice of materials marked a distinct change. Its pitched, resin-panel ceiling with timber veneer seemingly floats above oversized concrete piers. Its open walls dissolve the boundaries of the built space, creating an uninterrupted flow to the new surrounding terraces and concourse.

The project demonstrates how sensitive adaptive reuse, even on a small-scale like this, can catalyze physical improvement on a wider campus level. It provides UWS's inhabitants with a vibrant, high-quality amenity contributing to the formation of a collective campus core. Introducing a new layer of history to the site, the restored Boilerhouse with its monumental chimney now stands against the Greater Sydney skyline as a beacon of student activity.

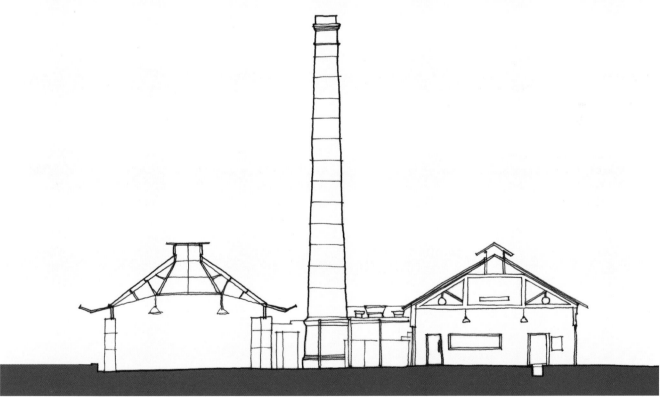

COMBINATION OF OLD AND NEW The 1894 boiler house was restored and linked via a modern kitchen to a new, semi-open pavilion.

BUILDING SECTION The new pavilion echoes its predecessor in its outline, but uses a twenty-first-century palette of materials.

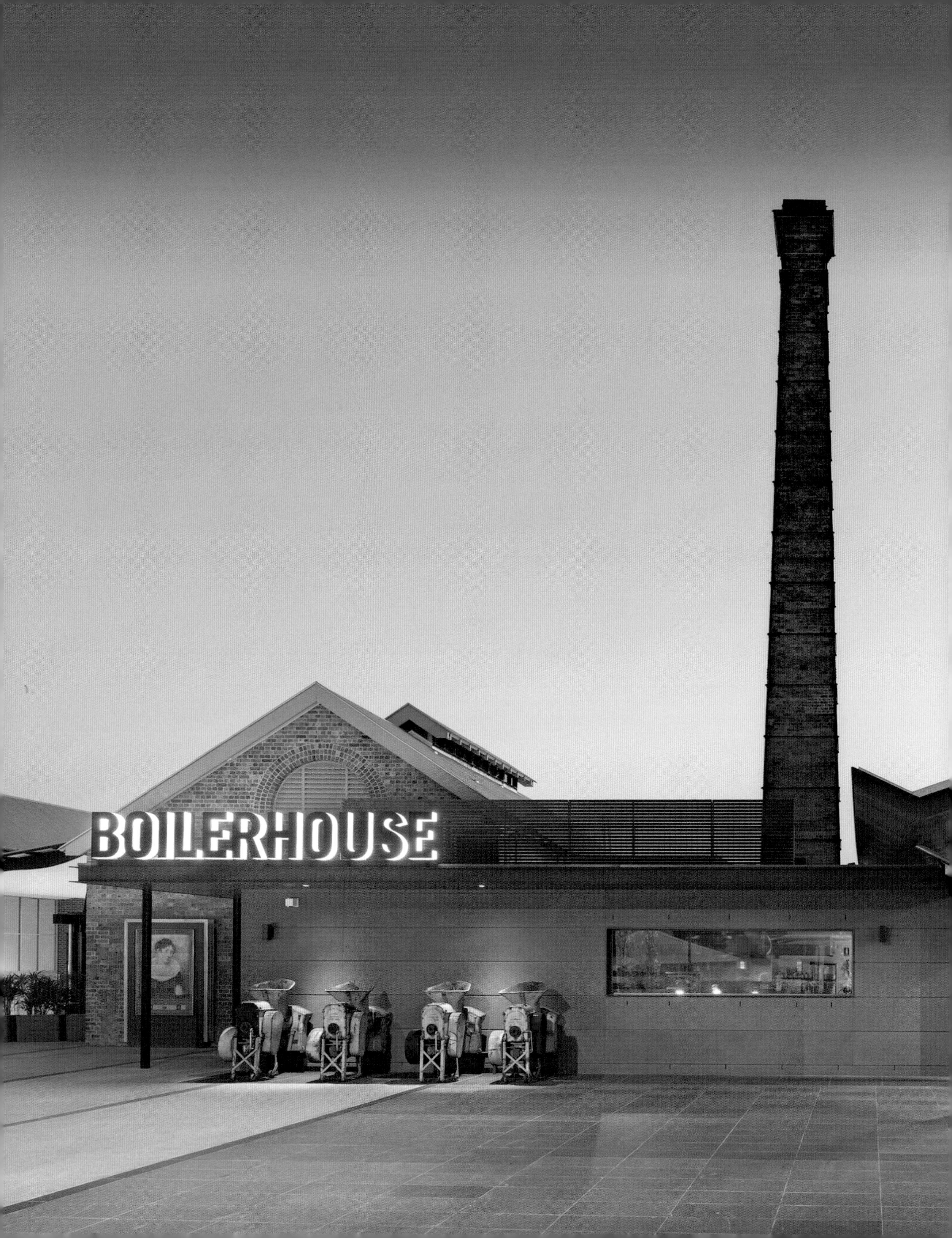
BOILERHOUSE

AN INDUSTRIAL LANDMARK The towering brick chimney dominates the site, acting as a beacon on campus to draw students and staff to this new focal point for university life.

TWO.TWO

STARCHITECTURE

BROAD ART MUSEUM
MICHIGAN STATE UNIVERSITY

Michigan, USA 2012 $40m 4,300m² (46,000ft²)
Architect: Zaha Hadid Architects

THE POLISHED, ANGULAR INTERIOR of the Broad Art Museum. A metal-clad, cantilevering staircase snakes vertiginously through the building's three floors.

WHEN ASKED FOR HIS CRITERIA FOR JUDGING THE COMPETITION ENTRIES FOR THE NEW ELI AND EDYTHE BROAD ART MUSEUM, ELI BROAD'S ANSWER WAS EMPHATIC: HE WANTED THE MOST ICONIC DESIGN, THE BIGGEST STATEMENT.[6]

Broad, the businessman, art collector and Michigan State University (MSU) alumnus, who provided $28 million in funding towards the $40 million project is no stranger to starchitect design; he has commissioned buildings by the likes of Renzo Piano, Richard Meier, César Pelli, and Frank Gehry. At Michigan State, the contest was won by Zaha Hadid Architects, a practice known for fluid geometries and exuberant, sculptural forms.

The Broad Art Museum is a potent demonstration of the spell that star names can weave upon donors; it is also an instance of big-name design and radical aesthetics being overtly employed to generate attention in pursuit of institutional goals. The museum was conceived as a cultural bridge between the university and the local community, integrating the one with the other whilst also investing both with artistic capital. Eli Broad has spoken of creating a 'mini-Bilbao effect', with Hadid's futuristic design drawing cultural tourists to the overlooked host city of East Lansing and raising MSU's profile.[7] The Broad, he said at the building's opening ceremony 'has the potential to do for Michigan State University and East Lansing what Frank Gehry's Guggenheim did for Bilbao, Spain'.[8] Museum officials expect to attract 125,000

to 150,000 visitors annually, boosting the regional economy by $5.75 million each year.

Sited on the campus's northern edge on a busy commercial thoroughfare, the Broad Museum has, in common with many university starchitect structures, a position as a gateway building. Despite a small footprint, its location ensures visibility and stimulates community engagement.

The building is radically different to any other structures in the locality. The contrast with the surrounding red-brick, Collegiate Gothic character of north campus is 'like a futuristic concertina pushing free from the deep pit of the devil's orchestra', writes the *Architectural Record*.[9] Its single trapezoidal volume is clad in a pleated and louvred steel skin of zigzagging angles. Its angled mass, almost truculent in tone, is accentuated by the angled louvres. The louvres themselves, in part supposedly a reference to the region's car industry, were motivated by a desire to screen the internal spaces to create a soft, filtered light within.[10] 'You get the sense that ZHA conducted this maniacal symphony because it could, cheered on by Broad and MSU, who will use the resulting big gesture as a calling card,' continued the *Architectural Record*. 'Nevertheless, respecting the scale of the neighbouring leafy Collegiate

Gothic red-brick quads and the commercial strip across the way, the building fits in.'[11]

As is often said of the museum creations of celebrity architects, the Broad blurs the line between contemporary art and the buildings designed to house it. Of its 4,300-square-metres (46,000-square-feet) of floor space, nearly two thirds is given over to gallery space. Each gallery is a different shape, a different size, with different lighting effects. Often tilting at hazardous angles, the walls of their rectilinear volumes must make for a challenging space for the museum's curators. A double-height café and education wing, and a twisting staircase which cantilevers dramatically through the centre of the two-storey building completes the interior. 'Like Hadid herself, the interior can't help but steal the limelight,' one critic has observed, 'and the building often becomes a more interesting place for looking back upon the building itself, instead of what is on the walls.'[12]

WEST FAÇADE The exterior is dressed in long steel fins that filter light into the galleries.

A GATEWAY BUILDING Envisaged as a gateway between MSU and East Lansing, the museum is sited on the northeastern edge of the red-brick campus.

THE EAST FAÇADE The building's pleated stainless steel and glass envelope has a 'prism-like quality' that Hadid has compared to 'a jewel box'.

DR CHAU CHAK WING BUILDING UNIVERSITY OF TECHNOLOGY, SYDNEY

Sydney, Australia 2012– Aus$180m 16,000m² (172,000ft²)
Architect: Frank Gehry

WHEN THE UNIVERSITY OF TECHNOLOGY, SYDNEY (UTS) UNVEILED DESIGNS FOR ITS NEW BUSINESS SCHOOL, ITS VICE-CHANCELLOR ANNOUNCED TO THE ASSEMBLED PRESS, 'WE'VE GOT THE OPERA HOUSE, AND IT'S HARD TO SAY WE ARE GOING TO BEAT THAT, BUT FROM WHAT I'VE SEEN WE'LL HAVE AN EQUALLY OUTSTANDING ICON'.[13]

THE NEW OPERA HOUSE UTS have high hopes that the business school will prove a city landmark.

Immediately, the national media heralded the campus's new building as a rival to the famed Sydney landmark. Why this hype for a university not known for its architectural endeavours?[14] Because the architect of the new building is Frank Gehry, the most well-known member of the starchitect cult and agent of the 'Bilbao effect'.

The Dr Chau Chak Wing Building, which commenced construction in 2012 (scheduled completion 2014), is just one of several projects recently built or underway at the UTS campus, located at the south end of the Central Business District. In 2008, the institution initiated a master plan process that will see an estimated Aus$1 billion spent over ten years to drastically reinvigorate its surroundings. It is the Dr Chau Chak Wing Building, though, which is commandeering all the attention.

Named after the Australian-Chinese businessman and philanthropist who donated Aus$20 million towards its construction, the new structure is rising on the site of an existing car park. For those expecting Gehry's trademark undulating free-form sculpture, a mix of hi-tech and frivolity, its design does not disappoint. Anticipated to accommodate nearly 1,300 students and over 300 faculty, its irregular exterior will feature two distinct façades. One, of undulating brick in sandstone colour, is intended to reference the earliest housing in the neighbourhood; the other, facing west, is composed of large, angled sheets of glass which fracture and mirror the cityscape. According to Gehry, the design is based upon a tree-house, reflecting 'a trunk and core of activity and...branches for people to connect and do their private work'.

The building has courted the inevitable controversy that accompanies a Gehry commission. Indeed, it has been a subject of spirited debate amongst local architectural cognoscenti since the designs were released. From Germaine Greer's 'imagine five brown paper bags with 15 windows cut in each side, scrunched up and then unscrunched and stacked together', to Alan Davies's 'microwaved chocolate castle', it has drawn a host of imaginative analogies. A familiar critique is that Gehry has delivered UTS with a design that is 'more about him than us, suggesting a boot-licking stance from a client that clearly defines its "needs" with "great dollops of global publicity"'.[15] Reflective not only of a backlash against universities engaging starchitecture as a marketing tool, this evaluation moreover reflects a widespread complaint that Gehry's buildings are a personal statement at the expense of context, placemaking and functionality. 'Notwithstanding some desultory references to local brick and sandstone building materials,' observed Davies, 'there isn't much of a sense of place to this building... It could be built pretty much anywhere.'

The glass expanses of the western elevation have prompted concerns of the usability of the building in the strong Australian afternoon sun.[16] Meanwhile, the eye-catching angles of its exterior have already sent projected costs spiralling from Aus$150m to $180m, as contractors grapple with the complexities of its undulating façade which necessitates five different types of brick.[17]

Commissioning a Gehry building is always something of a leap into the unknown. 'If I knew where I was going, I wouldn't do it,' Gehry has said. 'When I can predict or plan it, I don't do it.' For UTS, this brings risk but also adventure.

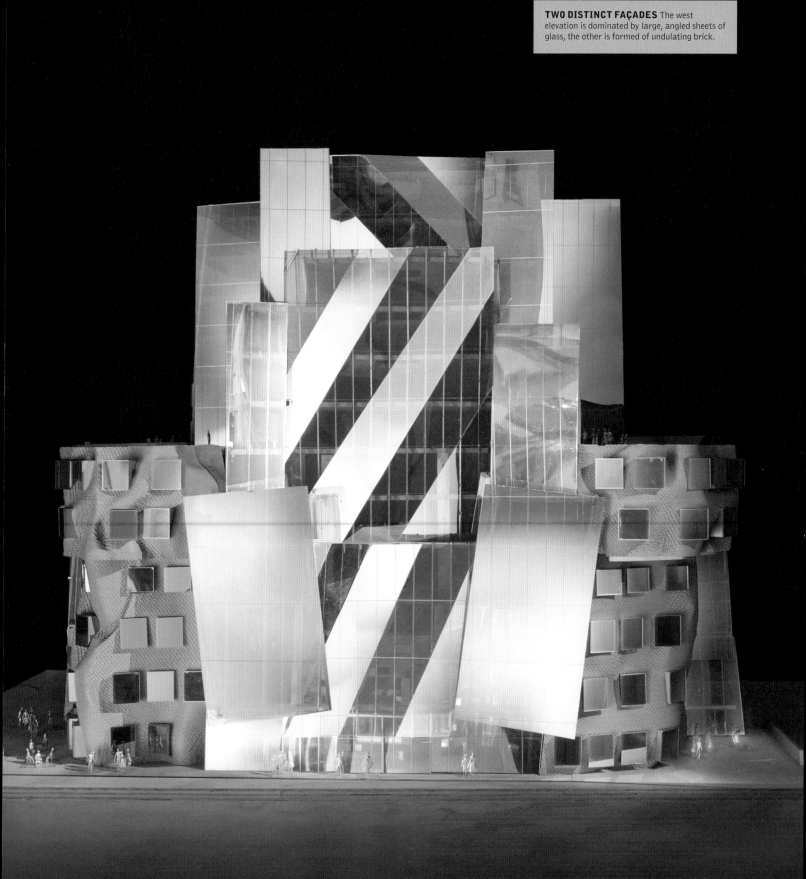

THE UNDULATING EAST FAÇADE The brickwork – which has earnt it the nickname of 'paper bag' – is an engineering challenge. An estimated 320,000 custom-designed bricks will be used.

LAW DEPARTMENT AND ADMINISTRATION BUILDING WIRTSCHAFTSUNIVERSITÄT WIEN

Vienna, Austria 2013 €29m 20,000m² (215,000ft²)
Architect: CRAB Studio

IN 2008, THE WIRTSCHAFTSUNIVERSITÄT WIEN (WU) UNVEILED A MASTER PLAN FOR A €500 MILLION NEW CAMPUS, WHICH WOULD UNITE THE HITHERTO SCATTERED URBAN INSTITUTION ONTO A SINGLE SITE FOR THE FIRST TIME.

RAINBOWS OF COLOUR The most colourful of the buildings that make up the new home of WU is Sir Peter Cook's Law Department and Administration complex.

Located in a rapidly growing district of Vienna, adjoining the 1,295-hectare (3,200-acre) Prater Park, the project was envisaged as the corporeal realization of a new era for the university. Necessitating huge investment, it was conceived as an opportunity for WU – Europe's largest university focusing on business and economics – to strategically reposition itself on a global stage. Bold contemporary architecture was, from the outset, envisaged as a foremost vehicle of expressing these twenty-first-century ambitions, and the newly completed campus now boasts a range of eclectic individual buildings by five international practices. Amidst this architectural bricolage, much of the spotlight has been devoted to Zaha Hadid's Library and Learning Centre. Arguably, however, it is a two-wing complex designed by Peter Cook's CRAB Studio that has proven the most eye-catching of the group.

Sir Peter Cook has been at the forefront of the global architecture field for over half a century. Best known for his founding role within Archigram, a group which dominated the architectural avant-garde in the 1960s, his work as a lecturer has made him a prominent voice around the world. It is only in more recent years, though, that his name has become known in wider circles with the construction of Graz's Kunsthaus (dubbed 'the friendly alien') and now with the striking new ensemble for WU.

Located on the southwestern portion of campus neighbouring the Prater Park, the pair of buildings house very different functions. One is home to the law faculty and related research institutes, while the other is the seat of WU's central administration. They are united, however, by an arresting use of vivid colour, imparting a cheering accent under Vienna's often-grey skies. While the buildings' ground-floor levels have largely closed façades, their upper levels are a blaze of polychromy. Coloured bands, ranging from dark orange to pale yellow, are striated across the elevations separated by windows. Slats of untreated Austrian larch – a hardwearing wood that gradually bleaches as it weathers – wrap around the structures horizontally, vertically, and diagonally, animating their surfaces further. The timber is intended to act as louvres, shading the interiors, while also acting as a visual link to the tree canopy of the Prater. Internally, the buildings are no less colourful: yellow window frames, brightly-painted walls, vibrant furniture.

In designing the buildings, Cook drew heavily from his own extensive experience of academia. Informal or extracurricular exchange that happens incidentally and surreptitiously is, he theorizes, the lifeblood of a university. Many years as a university lecturer had taught him that for this to happen collegiate buildings require social spaces in plentiful quantities, places that inspire their users and encourage them to linger after class has ended. This attitude is expressed in an unfolding architecture of passages, niches, roof terraces, and courtyards.

The organization of the law building into departments and sub-departments organically suggested an unwinding ground plan. The building's mass gently unfurls around several courtyards, snaking east to west along a 200-metre (650-feet) length. Balconies are periodically carved from its exterior, while internally pockets of informal space have been hewn amongst the necessary repertoire of offices and teaching spaces. The focal point of the scheme is the law library. Sited cocoon-like at the heart of the building, the elevation enwraps it while a stepped terrace forms its roof. Inside, special study booths that have been likened to floating nests survey the space from elevated heights.

As a whole, this is an engaging and social building set within a mosaic-like, dynamic campus that physically translates WU's ambitions to become Europe's foremost modern university.

- Seminar and Study Rooms
- Special Law Library
- Law Departments
- Research Department
- Administration
- Bakery

GROUND PLAN of the two-wing complex. The twisting building wraps around a central terraced courtyard.

OUTDOOR LANDSCAPES Particular attention has been paid to exterior spaces to encourage social encounters.

TWO.THREE

HUB BUILDINGS

THE FORUM
UNIVERSITY OF EXETER

Devon, UK 2012 £31m 9,000m² (97,000ft²)
Architect: Wilkinson Eyre Architects

LINK TO LIBRARY The façade of the existing library was cut out to open onto the Forum.

THE UNIVERSITY OF EXETER'S STREATHAM CAMPUS SUFFERED FROM A DRAWBACK SHARED BY MANY UK UNIVERSITIES – IT LACKED A CENTRAL CAMPUS FOCUS.

Constructed on an historic rural estate in the 1920s and 30s, it had grown incrementally in the 1950s, 60s, and 70s to a variety of master plans that resulted in a medley of buildings, many unexceptional. In 2006, the university began a reappraisal of this estate. It recognized that with tuition fees set to rise, student expectations would swell accordingly, making UK higher education increasingly more competitive and consumer orientated. Concurrently it was anticipating 5,000 extra students by 2026, bringing the total population to 16,000.[18] Against this backdrop, the university embarked upon an ambitious capital investment programme that would boost student satisfaction levels and, critically, steal a lead on its rivals. The jewel in the crown of these ambitions was the Forum, a multi-functional new campus gateway and centrepiece.

The brief given to the competition-winning architects, Wilkinson Eyre, in 2008 was by no means an easy one. Firstly, the structure had a multifarious functional remit: to house a large student services centre, 400-seat auditorium, teaching and seminar spaces, dining and retail facilities, informal study zones, and social areas. Secondly, the timeframe for completion was constrained by an unmoveable Royal opening, scheduled in 2012 as part of the Queen's Diamond Jubilee tour. Thirdly, it was to occupy a

demanding site, slotted between tired, rigid mid-century structures on steeply sloping land. The realized building, though, succeeded in rising to this suite of challenges.

Wilkinson Eyre's approach was to capitalize on Streatham's biggest asset – its natural setting. Its undulating landscape makes Exeter one of the greenest and most attractive campus universities in Britain. The Forum responds to this by adopting an organic plan covered by an all-embracing 'blanket' roof. The topography of the hillside has been rationalized into two circulation levels which link the existing library and Great Hall, hitherto divided by a sharp slope. At ground-floor level, the building encloses a column-free pedestrian street – effectively a high street for university life – lined with cafés, shops, a bank, break-out spaces, and access to the two-storey student services centre, auditorium, and library, the façade of which was cut out to allow entry. The upper floor connects the Great Hall and student services to a range of learning spaces and seminar rooms. The seminar rooms look onto an internal landscaped courtyard, while the upper deck features a rooftop terrace.

The roof itself ranks as one of the most eye-catching elements of the scheme. At over 3,200 square metres (35,000 square feet) it is the largest

continuous timber grid shell in the UK, and extends from the library, across the Forum, and around the Great Hall. The undulating, gridded canopy is formed of a series of triangular timber panels punctuated with glazing that dissolves the barriers between inside and out.[19] This organic, inside/outside character is sustained by an interior architecture of galleries, bridges, planting, and benches. Throughout, the Forum offers plentiful places to sit and gather, from the timber benches to study desks for informal learning.

For the first time, Exeter has a defined entrance to campus, one that combines social, learning, and service spaces in a loose-fit arrangement that offers flexibility for future changes. 'Its potential to transform not only individual day-to-day experiences but also the prospects of the university as a whole places it in a different league,' *Architecture Today* has praised. 'The Forum seems to be exactly the building that Exeter was missing and other UK universities...will be watching with interest and not a little jealousy.'[20]

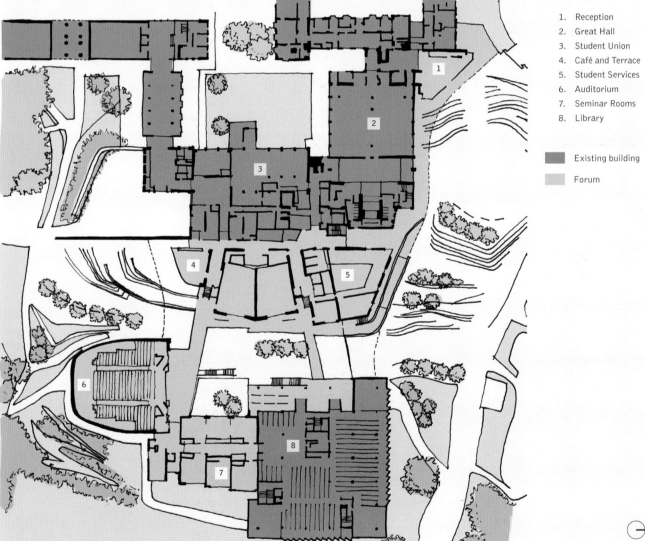

1. Reception
2. Great Hall
3. Student Union
4. Café and Terrace
5. Student Services
6. Auditorium
7. Seminar Rooms
8. Library

Existing building

Forum

STEPPED NORTH ELEVATION The steep terrain has been rationalized into two circulation levels that connect the library and Great Hall, hitherto divided by a slope.

UPPER LEVEL PLAN The Forum extends from the library, wraps around the Great Hall, and up to the new reception.

TIMBER GRID SHELL The timber and glass grid shell roof overhangs the Forum's entrance.

NEW FRONT DOOR The Forum creates a new main reception for the university, accessed via the new North Plaza.

INDOOR HIGH STREET A column-free pedestrian street runs through the building giving access to shops, cafés, library, auditorium, and courtyard.

HUB CENTRAL
UNIVERSITY OF ADELAIDE

Adelaide, Australia 2011 Aus$42m 10,500m² (110,000ft²)
Architect: HASSELL

AUSTRALIA AND NEW ZEALAND ARE AT THE FOREFRONT
OF THE TREND FOR HUBS – MULTIFUNCTIONAL CAMPUS
BUILDINGS THAT PROVIDE A WIDE-RANGING MIX OF SOCIAL
AND LEARNING SPACES.

TRANSFORMING STUDENT EXPERIENCE
A 24/7 learning-living facility that integrates
library, study booths, IT facilities, kitchen, and
resting niches.

Exemplifying this is the University of Adelaide's Hub Central. Far removed from the traditional, single-use structures that once dominated university construction, the Hub Central was conceived to be a place of many things for many people, that can adapt to weather future changes in the realm of higher education. Its three levels have resonated with student activity since its opening in September 2011. Spread over 10,500 square metres (110,000 square feet), it houses project rooms, lounges, information service areas, a self-service kitchen, computer stations and suites, retail and food outlets, plus the Maths Learning and Writing Centres. Furthermore, it is open 24 hours a day.

Situated in the cultural heart of the city, the University is an urban institution where vacant land is at a premium. Room was carved for the new building by recycling what was hitherto a barren but central courtyard, Hughes Plaza, framed by the main campus library, lecture rooms, and academic departments. These fundamental constituents of the campus are united through this connective campus heart, enclosed beneath a transparent roof that illuminates the space with natural daylight.

Essentially, Hub Central was created as a place of experimentation, a place that would foster new approaches to learning, communication, and interdisciplinary knowledge. Students have the flexibility to shape their own study environments, whether this be stretched out on the Hub's many beanbags or in the semi-secluded booths, with supporting facilities and services at their fingertips. The university's student-centric focus is best epitomized by its consultative design approach which sought to engage faculty and students. Over 9,000 hours of student involvement went into its creation as part of a reference group and on-going governance body working alongside the building's architects, HASSELL. This collaborative process had a distinctive impact upon the realized building, stimulating HASSELL to design from the 'inside-out' – wherein the fit-out design informed the basic building. An ideas wall erected outside the library elicited an abundance of feedback, and together with online surveys and social media, gave rise to such features as digital signage screens, for example, which display relevant community information and list computer availability.

This student-focused attitude is indicative of the increasing drive to deliver the best campus experience in the face of growing national and international tertiary-level competition. What is equally salient is that the Hub has the flexibility to respond to the changing parameters of student expectations in the future. The building is a highly malleable and ductile place. Its flexible floor plan currently includes training spaces, newsroom, de-stress zones, pop-up shops, and food areas which are purely temporal. Many of its interior fittings – sofas, stools, desks, mobile computers, miniature whiteboards – are on wheels or lightweight, allowing them to be easily moved, harmonizing with the flux of student life.

From its conception to its design, Hub Central is all about catering for the student, and so far they seem to be satisfied. Post-occupancy surveys put student approval ratings for the hub at 80 per cent.[21] Drop-in numbers to the Maths and Writing Centres increased by 470 per cent following its opening. It reflects changing patterns of undergraduate learning and interaction, it provides new connections across campus that bring the community closer together, and delivers students with a colourful new 'front door' to their university experience.

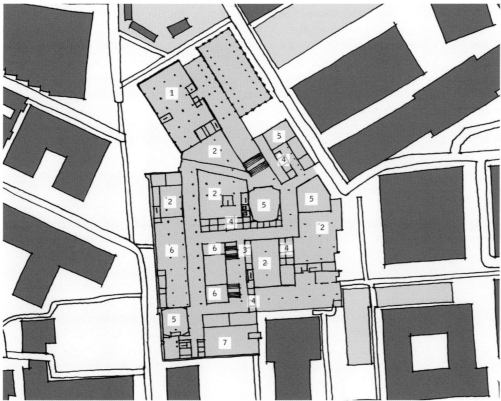

1. Existing Library
2. Collaborative Learning
3. Individual Learning
4. Project Space
5. Formal Learning
6. Retail
7. Learning Support

NEW STUDY ENVIRONMENTS 11 project booths are located on levels three and four.

LEVEL THREE PLAN The Hub covers 10,500 m² over three levels.

CAMPUS FRONT DOOR The Hub is an initial point of contact and first port of call for students.

STUDENT CENTRIC The design process was collaborative and student-centric, motivated by the desire to create the best student experience.

ERASMUS PAVILION
ERASMUS UNIVERSITY ROTTERDAM

Rotterdam, Netherlands 2013 €5.2m 1,800m² (19,400ft²)
Architect: Powerhouse Company/De Zwarte Hond

SINCE ITS FOUNDATION IN THE 1970s, THE WOUDESTEIN CAMPUS HAS GROWN IN PIECEMEAL FASHION. ALTHOUGH THE MAIN SITE OF ERASMUS UNIVERSITY ROTTERDAM (EUR), IT HAS LONG SUFFERED FROM ITS INCOHERENT, CLUTTERED LAYOUT AND INDIFFERENCE TO PLACE-MAKING.

GRAND CAFÉ OVERLOOKING PLAZA The building's glazed exterior shell creates a dialogue between inside and out.

In 2010, the institution's executive board set out to address this with the launch of a three-phase master plan to rationalize, modernize, and revitalize its Brutalist suburban estate.

With the objective of investing the austere campus with a sense of place, stage two of the project saw the completion of a new campus heart. At the intersection of the two main pedestrian axes of the plan, at Woudestein's natural centre of gravity, a plaza was constructed on an underutilized green area marred by parked cars. Creating a formal entry to the campus and public landscape, the plaza will upon build-out be the setting for student housing, a multifunctional educational building, underground car park, the renovated library, garden, and food outlets. The heart of the scheme – a student hub building – was completed in 2013.

The Erasmus Pavilion is conceived as the campus's social core, answering EUR's calls for a 'meeting place' that would act as a magnet for students, staff, and external visitors. A destination to relax, study, and engage, it is multifaceted in nature, typifying the 'hub' genre. Carved into the sloping terrain of the site, the two-storey building has multiple entrances allowing access from different sides at different levels. Those approaching from the south enter the foyer of a multi-purpose theatre, from where they descend a curving grey-tiled staircase into the ground-floor Grand Café spanning the

building's western façade. From the café, a walkway encircles the building, seamlessly adjusting to gradations in the terrain via stairs and ramps to lead to enclosed meeting rooms and study areas.

The layout is determined by what constitutes the building's most singular feature – the sculptural, red oak-clad box at the centre of the building's volume which contains the theatre. This flared box is suspended inventively from the upper level into the ground floor space. The foyer, café, study booths, and other public spaces furl around it. This organization stemmed from a pragmatic rationale. Locating this 'dark space' element in the interior enabled the exterior to be designed as a glazed box. Each elevation is an unbroken glass expanse, inviting passers-by to engage in the activities within. The sense of permeability between outside and in is two-fold. From within the pavilion, the users have panoramic views over the newly-created landscape. In summer, the glass walls of the café can be opened to extend the space onto the plaza terrace. All this glazing might easily have given the structure a stark, clinical mien, yet thanks to the flared wooden cube within this has been triumphantly avoided. The overhanging ceiling humanizes the volume's scale which, together with the warmth of the oak, produces a welcoming, intimate atmosphere. At night, this ambience is intensified through lighting effects. The red walls of the theatre box are illuminated and glow

through the timber panelling to create a physical metaphor for the pavilion as Woudestein's living, beating heart.

A thoughtful approach to light is visible throughout the building's design. The level of sunlight within the interior is checked by arcs of custom-designed aluminium louvres suspended across each façade. Using remote controls, occupants can thereby regulate light levels and also customize the level of openness of the building to the outside world depending on programmatic needs and the changing seasons. This is an example of the flexibility that pervades the design. The theatre – planned to host a range of lectures, debates, and performances – has a fully retractable stage built on wheels that allows the capacity of the hall to be increased; the foyer is suitable as a venue for graduation drinks and other events; and the study spaces can be enclosed to act as seminar rooms. The result is a dynamic and responsive building that acts as a glowing beacon for EUR. Ultimately, the most reliable evaluation for the pavilion's success is its popularity with the university and local community; bustling with activity and crowded with people, those wishing for a table in the café must fight for a seat.

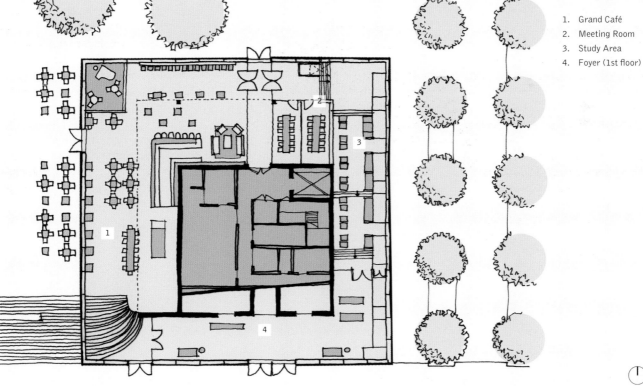

1. Grand Café
2. Meeting Room
3. Study Area
4. Foyer (1st floor)

NEW CAMPUS CORE The Pavilion is the focus of a revitalizing master plan, creating a central meeting point for students, faculty, and visitors alike.

GROUND FLOOR PLAN Study and social spaces wrap around the perimeter of the building. The theatre, accessible from the first floor, occupies the inner volume.

GLOWING HEART The interior timber casing of the theatre box is illuminated at night, creating a warm glow that radiates through the glass façades.

TWO.FOUR

INTERDISCIPLINARY SCIENCE RESEARCH BUILDINGS

SANFORD CONSORTIUM FOR REGENERATIVE MEDICINE UNIVERSITY OF CALIFORNIA, SAN DIEGO

California, USA 2011 $127m 14,000m² (150,700ft²)
Architect: Fentress Architects

FIVE WORLD-LEADERS IN LIFE SCIENCES RESEARCH ARE BROUGHT TOGETHER UNDER THE ROOF OF THIS FOUR-STOREY LABORATORY STRUCTURE.

TWO-STOREY BREAK ROOMS at each end of the building are shared between floors.

Scientists from the Salk Institute for Biological Studies, the Scripps Research Institute, the Sanford | Burnham Medical Research Institute, the La Jolla Institute for Allergy and Immunology, and the University of California, San Diego (UCSD), are united to pioneer the next generation of tools, therapies, and technologies in stem cell research. Dubbed the 'Collaboratory', the building that houses this ambitious project was planned from the outset to encourage the kind of collaboration and interaction between biologists, physicians, engineers, physicists, chemists, and computer scientists that has been revolutionizing scientific research in recent years.

Completed in 2011 after five years of planning, the centre houses laboratories, offices, and meeting rooms, plus a standalone café and auditorium separated from the main structure by a landscaped plaza. It sits on three hectares (7.5 acres) of UCSD land at the heart of San Diego's biotechnology cluster. Built adjacent to the UCSD campus and to Louis Kahn's celebrated Salk Institute, its designers, Fentress Architects, were working amidst an eminent design context. At the heart of their scheme lies the principle that governs this building typology: collaboration. The brief received from the Consortium's vice president was explicit: 'design a building that will enhance

communications between the best minds in biomedical research'.

Fentress responded to this instruction with a novel solution. In most buildings, whether laboratories or not, the various floors are disconnected. The Sanford Consortium building, however, is structured around vertical connections. Two-storey rooms were planned at either end of the building's length. These 'break-out' rooms connect researchers across different disciplines and floors in an informal setting. Similarly, staircases were sited in the middle of work areas linking floors visually and spatially and thus heightening proximity between its inhabitants. Essentially, their objective is to change the traditional behaviour patterns of scientists, drawing them out of the laboratories and creating an atmosphere auspicious for serendipitous interactions. The staircases were not merely considered to be utilitarian circulatory spaces, but envisaged as social spaces for informal communications and jotting down ideas on the writeboard walls. The interactive boards themselves are a means of stimulating the sharing of ideas: users write with their fingers instead of a marker pen, and can email the board's contents easily and quickly. The writeboards even amend poor handwriting.

The underlying intention behind these elements was to cause what the

Consortium calls 'creative collisions'. 'The design means that you can't walk from spot A to B to C without meeting other people,' according to Alan Trounson, president of the California Institute for Regenerative Medicine which contributed $43 million in public funds to the project. This collegial quality was enhanced by the amount of glass featured throughout the interior. Almost 280 square metres (3,000 square feet) of it are used, inviting awareness and interconnections both inward and outward.

Collaborative team research is not the only priority of the Consortium, however. It was also important that the building supported individual study. This the building does in its series of exterior office 'pods'. Cantilevered from a walkway and external to the main building envelope, these glazed pods cover the western elevation in a Jenga-like pattern. They constitute the most eye-catching aspect of the centre's fabric. 'Alone but connected', the pods afford the faculty space to do focused work whilst enjoying natural lighting and scenic views towards the Pacific Ocean. And in order to take advantage of cooling ocean breezes, the pods feature a relatively rare

WEST FAÇADE Office pods are cantilevered from exterior walkways on the north and west façades of the building.

GROUND PLAN LEVEL 2 One of the four storeys that make up this laboratory building within San Diego's biotechnology cluster.

occurrence – operable windows. Cutting edge research centres are not, in their nature, 'green' places. The high-tech, high-powered technologies that such institutes require are inherently energy-greedy. Nonetheless, the sustainability agenda did feature highly in many aspects of the project. Chilled beam technology cools the building using reclaimed water, bioswales in the car park filter and absorb storm water, and native plants are used in the landscaping.

The Sanford Consortium stands as an example that successful academic design is about more than aesthetics. With thoughtful planning, architecture can stimulate and nurture scientific research by acting as a catalyst for behaviour change.

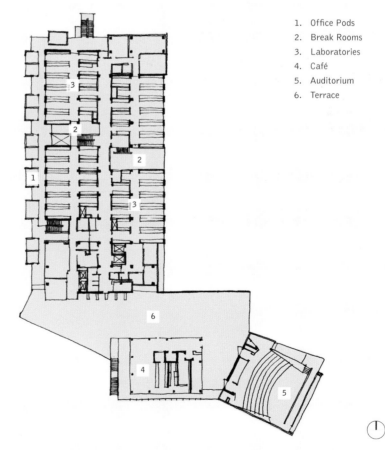

1. Office Pods
2. Break Rooms
3. Laboratories
4. Café
5. Auditorium
6. Terrace

THE WEST FAÇADE AT DUSK The colourful patchworth of cantilevered office pods provide space for individual study, away from the open-plan layout of the main volume of the building.

Opposite:
CHANCE MEETINGS AND COLLABORATION Break rooms are a focal point of the building, intended to break scientists out of private research.

MILLENNIUM SCIENCE COMPLEX
PENNSYLVANIA STATE UNIVERSITY

Pennsylvania, USA 2012 25,000m² (270,000ft²)
Architect: Rafael Vinoly Architects

AT THE EASTERN EDGE OF PENNSYLVANIA STATE'S SCIENCE DISTRICT, THE UNIVERSITY'S NEWEST HOME FOR CUTTING-EDGE SCIENTIFIC RESEARCH, THE MILLENNIUM SCIENCE COMPLEX (MSC), RISES UP LIKE THE PROW OF AN ENORMOUS SHIP.

CANTILEVERED NORTHWEST CORNER of the building has been likened to the prow of a ship.

Spurred by an institutional stratagem to foster new approaches to research, the opening of the MSC brought together two of the university's foremost centres – the Materials Research Institute and the Huck Institutes for Life Sciences – into a single building. It was one of the first buildings in the country erected specifically to integrate the physical and life sciences, and it was garbed in a fittingly unusual architectonic designed by internationally-renowned Rafael Viñoly Architects. The L-shaped building houses the institutes in two perpendicular wings, stretching 170 metres (550 feet) to the north and 135 metres (440 feet) to the west. The wings step up in a series of long, flat planes until they converge at the northwest corner where the building reaches its highest point, a dramatic 45-metre (150-feet) cantilever pierced by a vast light well.

The building's unconventional form was not a matter of mere aesthetics, but was designed to meet specific programmatic needs and to respect the campus's master plan principles. The cantilevering roof may serve as a monumental architectural landmark, but its raison d'être was to facilitate the pioneering research that goes on in the depths of the building. Nestled in an underground level between the MSC's two wings and encased within thick concrete slabs are the hi-tech 'quiet' laboratories, where state-of-the-art characterization and fabrication apparatus necessitate exacting vibration-free

conditions. The equipment is so sensitive that building-based vibrations may have affected it. The giant cantilever precluded this by ensuring there is no occupied space above the laboratories. Even the garden plaza that occupies this overhanging zone has been carefully landscaped to provide optimum conditions for the subterranean workspace. Garden paths meander around green plantings, deliberately placed so as to channel pedestrian traffic closer to the building edges to thereby minimize vibrations, while their surfaces are of loose gravel to further cushion impact and discourage skateboarders.

The open plaza, meanwhile, serves another function: supporting the master-plan goal to foster a pedestrian-friendly campus. As the largest academic building on campus, careful consideration was required to ensure the MSC respected the master plan values and extant physical setting. Its prodigious size might easily have rendered the building as a barrier to pedestrian circulation; instead it was conceived as a gateway to the university's science and research corridor from the east. The cantilever serves the role of a monumental archway. The stepped elevation of the wings from four storeys at its apex down to two storeys at the ends has the effect of scaling the building mass to its environment, specifically to the pedestrian-scale streetscape on its eastern side. Furthermore, its brick veneer creates a deep red colour palette which echoes the hues of the wider campus.

Internally, the MSC conforms to the generic interdisciplinary building's remit for flexibility and collaboration. Changes in the size and configuration of research teams are accommodated by large, continuous, and open laboratories; utilities are provided through an easily reconfigurable distribution system that can be quickly demounted and rearranged as research needs change. The distribution of the two resident institutes in the two separate wings means that the MSC places less emphasis on encouraging interaction between its researchers than many other interdisciplinary science buildings. Nonetheless, 260 square metres (2,800 square feet) of common space is provided in the form of conference and seminar rooms, kitchens, outdoor terraces, and social spaces to foster the kind of 'chance encounters' that breed the interdepartmental collaboration which lies at the heart of the MSC mission.

The MSC responds to a sensitive research programme and encases it within a vast, dramatic building form. It is a form in which visible and hidden design features work together in the service of cutting-edge science.

L-SHAPED BUILDING Its two wings have stepped levels featuring vegetated rooftops.

LANDSCAPED GARDEN A lightwell illuminates the carefully landscaped garden at the northwest corner of the MSC.

A GATEWAY BUILDING The MSC is intended to act as a gateway, by improving pedestrian circulation from central campus to its eastern portions.

THE BRAGGS
UNIVERSITY OF ADELAIDE

Adelaide, Australia 2013 Aus$96m 8,000m² (85,000ft²)
Architect: BVN Donovan Hill

THE UNIVERSITY OF ADELAIDE'S NEWEST SCIENCE BUILDING
SHIMMERS IN THE SUNSHINE. ITS FACETED GLASS EXTERIOR,
REFLECTING AND REFRACTING DAYLIGHT AS THE SUN MOVES
ACROSS THE SKY, IS NOT SIMPLY AN ARCHITECTURAL CONCEIT,
BUT A METAPHOR FOR THE WORK DESTINED TO TAKE PLACE INSIDE.

FIVE STOREY ATRIUM Informal gathering
spaces at its base and meeting rooms around it
encourage interaction.

The Braggs – named after the father and son winners of the 1915 Nobel Prize for Physics – is a cross-disciplinary research and teaching facility housing the Institute for Photonics and Advanced Sensing (IPAS). Light lies at the heart of the institute's pursuit – photonics. The discipline uses light to lead to discoveries across a wide scope of applications, engaging a translational methodology to do so – 'physics meets chemistry meets biology meets material science', according to the director of IPAS, Professor Monroe. Incorporating IPAS laboratories, a lecture theatre, and two floors of wet and dry laboratories for first-year undergraduates, the essential ideology of the building is to bring together researchers from across the scientific spectrum and to pique the incipient interest of the students as the scientists of the future.

Working within the stringent requirements of high-tech laboratory design, the building sets out to meet these objectives through its internal layout and relationship to the campus context. Located within the university's science and research precinct adjacent to the key green space of Maths Lawn, the Braggs encourages pedestrian traffic around and through it. Its striking entrance atrium, five storeys tall and flooded with natural light, responds to existing circulation routes from the street to the north and the lawn to the south and thereby encourages pedestrian movement through it. All the building's users – whether faculty, students, or researchers – use this space to access the facility. The atrium's ground-floor café, casual gathering areas, and flanking meeting rooms are designed to harness this footfall by encouraging informal encounters and dialogue.

The entrance atrium is one of two vertical 'streets' that shapes the interior organization. The other, stretching 50 metres across the Braggs's transparent southern façade, rises seven storeys high supported by a structural steel framework. Envisaged as a veranda, it not only provides a physical link between the levels but, through its picture-window panoramas over Maths Lawn, also visually connects the occupants with wider campus life. This sense of openness is fundamental to the building's mission to foster interconnections. The focus on transparency is evident not only in the provision of external vistas, but also in the views over the atrium enabled through glazed internal partitions.

Glass is a cornerstone of the building's design. Its crystalline elevations are composed of pleated patterns of vertical glass and solid panels – the latter tinted a warm-red hue to contextualize with the brick of the early campus architecture – distributed relative to orientation. The north façade combines both glass and solid panels with fixed sunbreakers to protect against the glare of the sun, while its southern counterpart is entirely glazed.

The building's concertina-like envelope is immediately eye catching. What passers-by may not recognize is that the angles of the facets on each storey are cut at varying degrees in accordance with the different wavelengths of refracted light that make up the light spectrum. Nevertheless their attention cannot fail to be caught by its glistening surface. And as for the tenants inside, The Braggs stands out as a tailored response to their needs, activities, and philosophy.

FOLDED FACETED FAÇADE The solid red panels of the eastern elevation refer to the surrounding brick buildings.

SOUTH ELEVATION The crystalline glass envelope of the southern façade makes for a strong presence and symbolizes the advanced photonics work occurring inside.

TWO.FIVE

JOINT-VENTURE BUILDINGS

AMSTERDAM UNIVERSITY COLLEGE
UNIVERSITY OF AMSTERDAM / VRIJE
UNIVERSITEIT AMSTERDAM

Amsterdam, Netherlands 2012 €9m 5,800m² (62,500ft²)
Architect: Mecanoo

TO THE EAST OF AMSTERDAM'S HISTORIC CITY CENTRE LIES
THE AMSTERDAM SCIENCE PARK, ONE OF EUROPE'S LARGEST
SCIENCE HUBS AND AN EXAMPLE OF JOINT-VENTURE
DEVELOPMENT ON A EXPANDED SCALE.

INTERACTION AND OPENNESS Academic
spaces and social areas are intermingled
throughout the building, while glazed partitions
create transparency.

Founded in 1996, it is owned by the University of Amsterdam (UvA), the City of Amsterdam, and the Netherlands Organisation for Science Research. It currently hosts UvA's Faculty of Science, several world-class research institutes, 120 companies and start-ups, sports centre, and residences, and, since 2012, has housed the new home of the Amsterdam University College (AUC). The Mecanoo-designed building of the AUC is an example of a joint-venture building on a joint-venture campus. The AUC was established in 2008 as a collaborative venture between the UvA and Vrije Universiteit Amsterdam (VU), the city's two largest higher education institutions, to provide an interdisciplinary syllabus taught fully in English that would advance Amsterdam's aspirations to become a world centre for research and development in the natural sciences. The new building is the physical manifestation of a shared programme between the two institutions.

The AUC, alongside the historic Anna Hoeve Farmhouse, forms the gateway to the Science Park. Intended to house all AUC's functions and all its 700 students (with a provision for a total population of approximately 900), its architects were given a multifaceted remit. They delivered a structure that combines an intensive curriculum of study with the cultural and social life of a campus. Over

four storeys, the building contains academic spaces – classrooms, library, project rooms, conference rooms, and workstations – alongside social and recreational spheres – restaurant and common room. These dual functions are not physically separated, but are mixed throughout the volume. The entrance leads to an open core in which stairs move past various study and sitting areas. Teachers' offices are conspicuously located alongside the communal spaces, while their glazed façades engender an atmosphere of community and transparency. In line with the college's interdisciplinary programme of study, the building places an emphasis on stimulating communication amongst its users. Thus, the wide staircase that rises from the ground-floor communal volume has double-height treads to function as tiered seating, thereby engaging the 'meeting in the hallway' topos. 'You should be able to study on the stairs as well as in the seminar rooms,' lead architect Francine Houben reflected.[22]

This objective is aided by the openness and commodiousness of the interior. The building is bathed in natural light. Key areas, such as the restaurant are illuminated with vast picture windows, while three voids tunnel daylight throughout the internal spaces and allow visual connection between the different floors. The largest of these voids sits at the heart of the building,

creating double-height expanses for the restaurant, common room, and study hall. Perhaps the most popular volume, however, is the intimacy of the attic-like study area and library nestled beneath the tilting roof.

The folding, zigzag roofline is the most distinctive aspect of the scheme. While drawing upon historic Dutch pitched roofs, it reinterprets this tradition with a playful twist. Its sedum surface provides a vivid colour that counterpoints with the structure's striking façade. Each elevation is clad in vertical panels of rusted Corten steel, emitting a warm glow that contrasts with the business-like architecture found throughout much of the Science Park. The panels are punctuated with a lively rhythm of windows of varying dimensions.

Both outside and in, the building thus far has answered the demands of this new collaborative enterprise. Its spirited exterior immediately invested the fledgling college with a unique physical identity, while inside its surprising range of spaces has enabled the convergence of a diversity of educational functions.

INTERNAL ATRIA Large, irregular voids bring daylight into the building and create relationships between the different levels.

BUILDING SECTION The folding, zigzag profile of the roof creates a top storey of intimate attic spaces.

RUST-RED CORTEN AND GREEN ROOF
The Corten façade and sedum roof are a
splash of colour that enlivens the environment
of the Amsterdam Science Park.

THE HIVE
UNIVERSITY OF WORCESTER

Worcester, UK 2012 £35.8m 13,250m² (142,600ft²)
Architect: Feilden Clegg Bradley Studios

THE HIVE WAS BORN OF A MUTUAL NEED FOR LIBRARY SERVICES.
IN 2004, WORCESTER COUNTY COUNCIL FOUND THEIR LIBRARY
FACILITIES NO LONGER FIT FOR PURPOSE; SIMULTANEOUSLY
THE UNIVERSITY OF WORCESTER WAS PLANNING A NEW CITY
CAMPUS AND LOOKING TO UPGRADE ITS LEARNING RESOURCES.

GOLDEN SKIN OF COPPER ALLOY Panels are
laid in a Herringbone diaper pattern to create a
glittering, reptilian surface.

The stage was set for a ground-breaking experiment in UK library development, which finally came to fruition in 2012 with the opening of the Hive, Britain's first fully-integrated, co-managed university and local authority library.

Located on a brownfield site adjacent to the River Severn, the building forms a physical intermediary between the city centre and the developing Castle Street campus beyond. Intended as the centrepiece of a wider scheme to rejuvenate a run-down part of Worcester, its exterior certainly brings some glitz to the area. Big and bold, the Hive is dominated by its roofline – a series of seven rectilinear cones of different heights and breadths clad in glittering copper-aluminium alloy. The effect has been described as that of golden exclamation points punctuating Worcester's medieval and Victorian skyline. The roof's eye-catching form draws inspiration from the immediate setting – the shape of the kilns of the historic Royal Worcester pottery works and the ridged terrain of the nearby Malvern Hills. More pragmatically, though, the cones are also a response to the need to break up the substantial massing and create height for ventilation.

The cones sit upon a four-storey box, large in plan and section. Its size is a reflection of the building's complex function. To answer its purpose as a dual-purpose facility, the building had to accommodate a diverse range of activities, including the academic and public library, county archives and records office, local history centre, archaeology service, café, and council customer services centre. The result is that the building is composed of a comprehensive mix of spaces, from public zones such as the entrance atrium and café to individual spheres such as meeting rooms and private study areas.

The interior volumes are softer, more muted, more humane than the exterior, and are characterized by natural light and timber. The main entry leads to a full-height atrium, sitting at the centre of the building directly below the soaring heights of one of the roof cones. The seven cones reflect much of the organization of the interior space. The underside of each is a timber-lined shaft crowned by a glazed opening which permeates the interior with daylight, investing the library with an ethereal calm. This is particularly apt in the quiet top-floor reading rooms, where the attic-like volume is defined by the sloping ceilings.

As with many libraries, the Hive becomes quieter as you scale its floors. During the design stage, university staff expressed concerns about the presence of the large children's library and noise problems associated with this. Such issues were addressed by the vertical organization of the building. The more bustling zones of activity – children's library, council services, 'quick picks' section of the library – are located on lower floors, while amenities requiring greater seclusion and concentration – the main library, meeting rooms, and study areas – are set on progressively higher levels.

Bringing together the needs of the two clients – university and local authority – and the various user groups that operate within them was always going to prove a design challenge. Yet, the Hive demonstrates that the model can work in particular circumstances. Clothed in a garb that redefines the conventional library architectonic, it is a promising response to the constraints of creating new libraries in an age when many are facing closure due to funding cuts.

1. Library / Study
2. Meeting Rooms
3. Children's Library
4. Youth Library
5. Archive
6. Quick Access

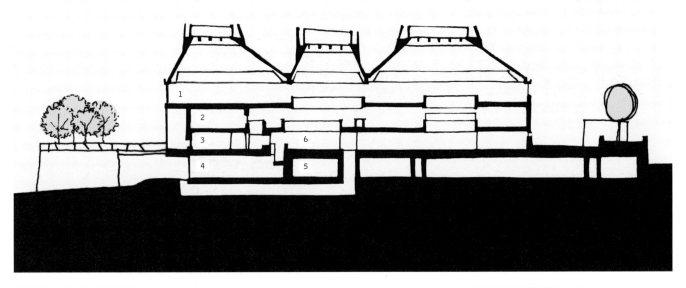

NORTH-EAST ELEVATION The Hive is intended to be a regional resource, aimed to be of value to the whole community.

BUILDING SECTION A wide variety of spaces and functions had to be incorporated to satisfy both council and university.

TOP-LIT ATRIUM The roof cones flood interior spaces in an even diffuse light.

NEW PUBLIC REALM The development includes
extensive new hard and soft landscaping.

UNIQUE SILHOUETTE The roofline echoes the
Malvern Hills and Worcester kilns.

HEALTH SCIENCES EDUCATION BUILDING UNIVERSITY OF ARIZONA / NORTHERN ARIZONA UNIVERSITY

Phoenix, USA 2012 $187m 25,000m² (270,000ft²)
Architect: CO Architects/Ayers Saint Gross

FOR MANY YEARS, PHOENIX WAS THE ONLY MAJOR CITY IN THE US WITHOUT AN ACADEMIC RESEARCH HOSPITAL OR MEDICAL SCHOOL. IN 2004, THIS SHORTAGE WAS ADDRESSED WITH THE CREATION OF THE PHOENIX BIOMEDICAL CAMPUS (PBC).

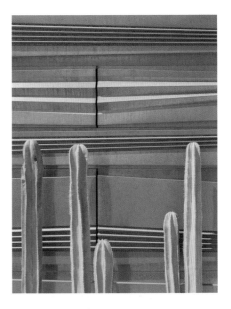

BURNISHED COPPER SKIN 26 types of copper are used on the façade to evoke earth strata of the regional landscape.

The 11-hectare (28-acre) downtown medical and bioscience precinct planned to host over 50,000 square metres (550,000 square feet) of research, academic, and clinical facilities was realized by the joint efforts of the city, the state of Arizona, Arizona State University, and the University of Arizona (UA). Central to the project was the inauguration of a new UA College of Medicine on the site, 115 miles north of its institutional base in Tuscon.

The PBC has steadily expanded ever since, notably with the opening in 2012 of the Health Sciences Education Building (HSEB). The new building enables the UA College of Medicine to expand its annual student intake. Its full objective, however, is far more expansive. The HSEB was constructed as a joint venture between the UA and Northern Arizona University (NAU) as an educational and research space that fosters the development of interdisciplinary clinical care and teaching, serving students and faculty of the UA College of Medicine-Phoenix, the UA College of Pharmacy, and the NAU College of Allied Health Sciences. The building is the physical proclamation of the collaboration and union of programmes from two universities with distinct institutional cultures, which it houses within a distinctive architectural shell.

The building is a product of two narratives: its programmatic functions and its topographical setting amidst Arizona's dramatic canyon formations and arid desert climate. Breaking away from the sterile mould of many science buildings, it is no rectangular cube. Its eccentric profile is characterized by a skewed ground plan and angular fissures sliced through its elevations, evocative of desert land formations. This metaphor is extended to its building materials. Clad in 26 varieties of burnished copper, the façade imaginatively reinterprets the stratified earth layers of the Southwest landscape. Wrapping around the exterior, the metal skin is bent, pressed, and perforated. The building's footprint is defined by two academic wings, which frame a tall, narrow space – a 'canyon'. Shaped to maximize self-shading and protected by a tensile canopy, the canyon acts as a courtyard and, together with the façade's staggered fissures, brings natural light into the heart of the structure.

The need to exploit yet control Arizona's harsh sunlight informed much of the building's design. Its east-west orientation ensures minimal heat gain, while façades are shaded with overhangs and vertical fins. Its western side extends northwards as a canopy over the floor-to-ceiling glazed wall of the main entrance and café.

Internally, the HSEB's functional objectives come into play. The building's interactive planning process involved input from the cross-section of health disciplines across both institutions and its layout reflects the growing trend within medical schools for interdisciplinary syllabi and small class sizes. Over six storeys, the building accommodates a combination of flexible classrooms, laboratories, clinical examination suites, library, offices, student lounges, and café. As reflects current practice, the disciplines are brought together rather than segregated. Future construction on the PBC will see the HSEB connected to new research buildings via shared public spaces, which, it is anticipated, will enhance cross-community interaction.

By combining a set of highly-specific, joint-venture objectives with an architectural symbolism drawn from the mountains of Arizona, the HSEB is a striking example of an interdisciplinary vision of higher education.

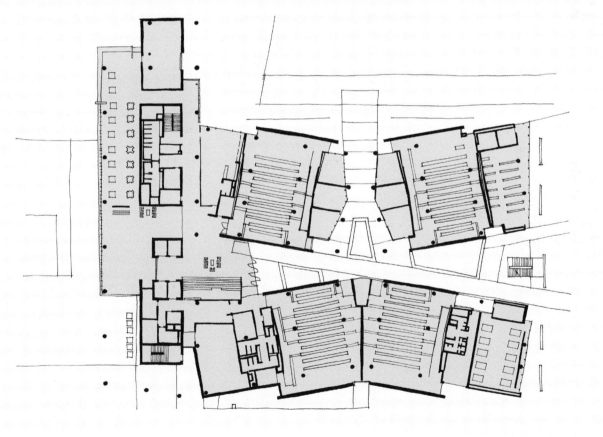

WEST FAÇADE The building serves the students and faculty of the University of Arizona and Northern Arizona University.

GROUND PLAN The building is divided into two six-storey wings.

EAST ELEVATION Inspired by the Southwest's canyon landscape, angular fissures slice through the façade.

TWO.SIX

NEW UNIVERSITIES BEYOND THE WEST

MASTER PLAN
DENIS SASSOU NGUESSO POLYTECHNIC UNIVERSITY

Kintele, Republic of the Congo 2013– 190 ha (470 acres)
Master planner: IAD

CONGOLESE HIGHER EDUCATION IS PLAGUED WITH MANY DIFFICULTIES – FAILING INFRASTRUCTURE, POOR TRAINING, LIMITED ACCESS, INADEQUATE STATE FUNDING.

MODULAR AND GEOMETRIC Structural elements are simple and repetitive to lower construction costs.

The recent presence of international investors and associated potential for fiscal growth in future decades is, however, slowly bringing change. A tangible manifestation of this is the inauguration of a new university, the Denis Sassou Nguesso Polytechnic, part of the government's initiative to facilitate access to tertiary learning and nurture a new generation of professionals that will strengthen the national and West African economy. Developed through a public-private partnership, the campus was designed in 2012–13 and is currently under construction.

Master planners IAD were presented with a 190-hectare (470-acre) plot situated alongside the River Congo on the northern edge of the capital Brazzaville, in the town of Kintele. Their design – devised for a maximum student population of 30,000 students – was conditioned by three decisive elements: the site itself, the need to keep construction costs realistic, and a desire to build responsibly. The location was selected on account of its proximity to a main road, the minimal need for deforestation, and the scenic views across to the nearby river. However, the land posed challenges, specifically in terms of its sloping gradient. IAD responded by envisioning a 'low-tech' campus organized around two perpendicular axes. The building platforms of its 25 constituent structures respond and adapt to the natural terrain.

Once completed in 2016, the campus will include sports facilities, library, 10 science and teaching buildings, and four university service buildings, set amongst tropical planting and a generous provision of plazas and lawns. Articulating a contemporary and international architectonic was of consequence to the client, and the campus's collection of low-rise buildings – four storeys at most – are sleek and unfettered in outline. The rectangular building units are arranged around a basic, interlocking geometry. In this, and in many other aspects of the plan, simplicity was seen as the design solution to accommodating the reality of the project's limited finances.

Throughout, the master plan is characterized by standardized materials and technically-accessible systems. Notably, this is seen in the modular, repetitive building components, as exemplified by the chain of monumental uniform lintel arches in the Olympic-sized swimming pool which form a superstructure from which an undulating ETFE roof is suspended. Furthermore, notwithstanding Kintele's equatorial climate, closed air-conditioned roofs were actively eschewed wherever possible in favour of naturally ventilated spaces coupled with adiabatic cooling panels. The semi-open swimming pool building again demonstrates this doctrine. Particularly in the student residences, draught

chimneys are being installed to enable ventilation. These simple methods are not only cost-efficient to install but also mediate the environmental footprint that such a large construction project inevitably carries.

Responsible development was fundamental to the ideology of the project. Accordingly, the campus plan incorporates a roll call of energy-efficient measures, including solar panels for water heating, and rainwater collection and grey-water treatment for maintenance and gardening. While sustainability is a buzzword in nearly all forms of construction, enforcing the concept was recognized as having specific potency because of its West African location. Building in this third-world yet growing region carries special accountability. Such schemes in effect will set the tone for future development. By applying a catalogue of low-tech and often ancient practices, the master plan thus delivers a formula for meeting the challenges of the African context in terms of cost, climate and sustainability.

A LOW-RISE LANDSCAPE Low-rise buildings interlock within hard and soft landscapes.

LOW-TECH SUSTAINABILITY Green roofs, rainwater collection, and draft chimneys rank amongst the 'green' features.

AERIAL RENDERING Buildings are positioned along two perpendicular axes and are organized on a simple interlocking geometry.

MASTER PLAN
SINGAPORE UNIVERSITY OF
TECHNOLOGY AND DESIGN

Singapore 2011– 7.7 ha (19 acres)
Master planner: UNStudio

SINGAPORE IS BROADENING ITS HIGHER EDUCATION PROVISION
AT RAPID PACE. 2009 SAW THE INAUGURATION OF ITS FOURTH
UNIVERSITY, THE SINGAPORE UNIVERSITY OF TECHNOLOGY AND
DESIGN (SUTD), ENVISAGED AS A NEW MODEL OF HIGHER EDUCATION
INSTITUTION FOR THE REGION.

SINGAPORE'S FOURTH UNIVERSITY The
SUTD will be a driver of technological innovation
and economic growth.

SUTD is a partnership of East and West, formed in collaboration with one of the leading universities in the West – MIT – and one of China's most prestigious institutions, Zhejiang University. After a multi-disciplinary first-year grounding in mathematics, sciences, humanities, and the arts, students will then specialize in four domain areas or 'pillars': Architecture and Sustainable Design, Engineering Product Development, Engineering Systems and Design, and Information Systems Technology and Design. Conceived to drive technological innovation and economic growth, this curriculum will be delivered around vital twenty-first-century competencies – teamwork, critical thinking, and communication skills. This mission is having tangible impact upon the guise that its physical estate is taking.

Sandwiched between the island's Changi airport and business park, the campus is organized along two key axes – the living and learning spines – which converge upon a central plaza, anchored on each corner by major academic buildings housing one of the four 'pillar' disciplines. Conceived for a projected student population of 5,000, the master plan engages a network of horizontal, diagonal and vertical vistas to enable SUTD's community to see, meet and communicate with each other through a nexus of crossing points. The most important of these

is the learning spine. The learning spine, stretching from the underground transit station at one edge to the business park at the other, is lined with student facilities, retail, and food outlets and connects the main academic and research buildings. The first stage of construction, comprising three academic buildings and two residential blocks, is due for completion by the close of 2014, to be followed by phased development as the academic population grows.

While Zhejiang has pledged to coordinate some courses, provide internship opportunities, and conduct joint research, it is with MIT that SUTD's closest ties lie. MIT has been involved at every stage of the fledgling university's formation, from developing its brief, to writing its curriculum, and faculty recruitment. While the architecture and layout of the Singapore site will differ dramatically from MIT's Boston campus, similarities are at work. Notably this exists in the 24/7 nature of the campus. The master plan brings together a rich and dense blend of building functions to ensure cultural and intellectual vibrancy, even after lessons end. Unlike Singapore's three older universities, SUTD is committed to fusing teaching and learning components into residential life. A high proportion of its students and faculty are envisaged to be resident, while within the residential

blocks themselves are scattered pods and voids to create places for community interaction and recreation.

This application of mixed-use design ideology is critical to achieving SUTD's ambitions for delivering an interdisciplinary, collaborative education. The integration of academic facilities, housing, and social buildings connected via open spaces and plazas is intended to foster the innovation and interchange that SUTD hopes to become renowned for. The question of how to incorporate these open spaces has, however, been a concern of both university administrators and architects. In the tiny island nation, acreage is necessarily at a premium and Singaporean campuses have recurrently struggled to include green-space provision. At SUTD, this challenge is increased since buildings are limited to eight storeys because of its proximity to Changi airport. Its designers, though, have responded with several innovative solutions. Ground-floor spaces are conceived as open-plan atria, allowing for climate-controlled green space. Green roofs are a signature feature, both as a method of environmentally-friendly

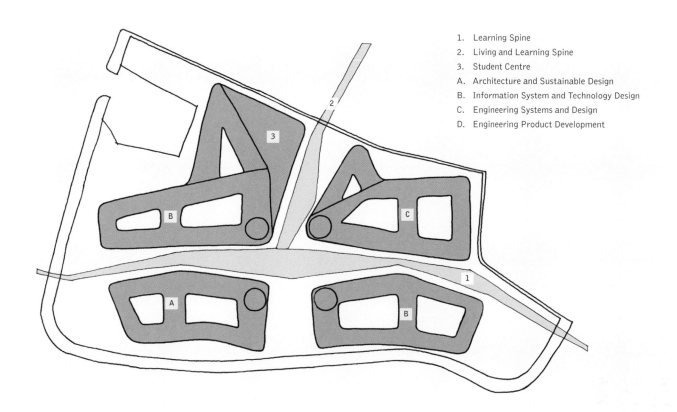

1. Learning Spine
2. Living and Learning Spine
3. Student Centre
A. Architecture and Sustainable Design
B. Information System and Technology Design
C. Engineering Systems and Design
D. Engineering Product Development

FOUR ACADEMIC PILLARS SUTD's master plan and curriculum is structured around four academic disciplines.

TWO MAIN SPINES The campus is organized around two cardinal axes: the living and learning spines.

cooling and as a means of extending the usable portion of the campus footprint. And while the university does have ground-level sports pitches, athletic facilities are encompassed into the building fabric and landscapes. The tennis court, for example, sits on the roof of the sports hall.

Planning for such a complex and ambitious range of functions in this tropical, highly-constrained environment is no mean feat. Yet early indications for the realized campus bode well. Reflecting SUTD's distinctive mission, its master plan pursues the idea of education as more than an academic level of study, but one designed to nurture social experience and intellectual innovation.

24/7 INTERACTION AND EXCHANGE
A network of horizontal, vertical, and
diagonal vistas enables SUTD's members to
see, meet, and communicate with one another.

MASTER PLAN
UNIVERSIDADE AGOSTINHO NETO

Luanda, Angola 2013 (phase 2) 2,000 ha (5,000 acres)
Master planner: Perkins + Will

FOLLOWING 27 YEARS OF CIVIL WAR, ANGOLA IS GROWING IN
SIZE, AFFLUENCE AND AMBITION, AND ITS GOVERNMENT IS
INVESTING IN ITS SOCIAL INFRASTRUCTURE. CENTRAL TO THE
OBJECTIVES OF ITS NATIONAL DEVELOPMENT PLAN IS THE
IMPROVEMENT OF HIGHER EDUCATION PROVISION.

FOUR-STOREY LIBRARY LOBBY Interiors are
shaded with aluminium louvres, which control the
intensity of the natural light.

The roots of Universidade Agostinho Neto extend back as far as 1975. Up to 2009, it was the country's only public university, existing as several separate campuses scattered across the country and thus unmanageable in size. In that year, the government effected a comprehensive overhaul of Agostinho Neto, breaking the oversized system into several individual universities and re-establishing Agostinho Neto itself as a smaller, single-site institution in the capital city, Luanda. For this new beginning, the state commissioned a brand new campus from US-based master planners and architects Perkins + Will. The 2,000-hectare (5,000-acre) greenfield savannah site on the southeast fringe of Luanda presented a blank slate to create a physical identity for Angolan higher education, to which Perkins + Will responded by imagining a campus entwined firmly with its local context. The driving force of this was the equatorial climate.

The first two phases of construction, completed in 2011 and 2013, have realized over 100,000 gross square metres (one million gross square feet) of a planned 1.5 million square metres (16 million square feet) projected to span six development stages and grow to accommodate 40,000 students. It was important to the architects that the new campus did not have to wait until it reached build out before it achieved a sense of institutional community. The

master plan, therefore, takes the form of a pinwheel, with core functions – library, refectory, student union – at the centre and specialized colleges organized in quadrangular fashion along orthogonal promenades. The first two phases realized the academic core and four science faculties (reflecting the university's academic bias), while future construction will see further faculties and housing added along the 'spokes'.

The central library serves as the hub of the campus. Shaped like an 'r', its lobby and administrative offices are housed in a five-storey tower, from whose top floor projects a glazed volume housing the reading rooms supported by a robust piloti. The debt here to Luanda's Modernist built heritage is clear, but another motive is also at work. The library's raised volume permits cooling airflow across to the faculty blocks on its leeward side, demonstrating the plan's commitment to creating a comfortable microclimate through passive means. The library is, in fact, the only structure with air conditioning installed; the others rely on a repertoire of traditional cooling methods to limit solar gain and promote cross-breezes.

To take advantage of the prevailing southwesterly winds, the whole campus is tilted from its north–south grid by 19 degrees. An angled roof, spanning the blocks and courtyards in-between, reduces the air pressure above the

buildings, which in turn draws hot air up and out through operable louvres. The roof canopy covers a continuous, shaded pedestrian network across the campus that connects the two to three-storey buildings via elevated walkways. The buildings are, for the most part, one room deep with a corridor to buffer the harshest sunlight. Façades are united by the common motif of aluminium louvres, which allow natural light into the rooms whilst also shading and minimizing dust.

The master plan, therefore, has sought to deliver a low-maintenance, low-cost, and sustainable vision for the new campus to answer the needs of Luanda's challenging climatic and economic conditions. 'The new campus is a catalyst for growth and development and is a symbol of the country's commitment to education,' praised Maria Manuela Ferraz of the Ministry of Construction. But, as a template for low-tech, low-energy university communities, it is moreover a model that has relevance beyond Angola's local circumstances, that can speak to all equatorial developing nations looking to expand their higher education infrastructure.

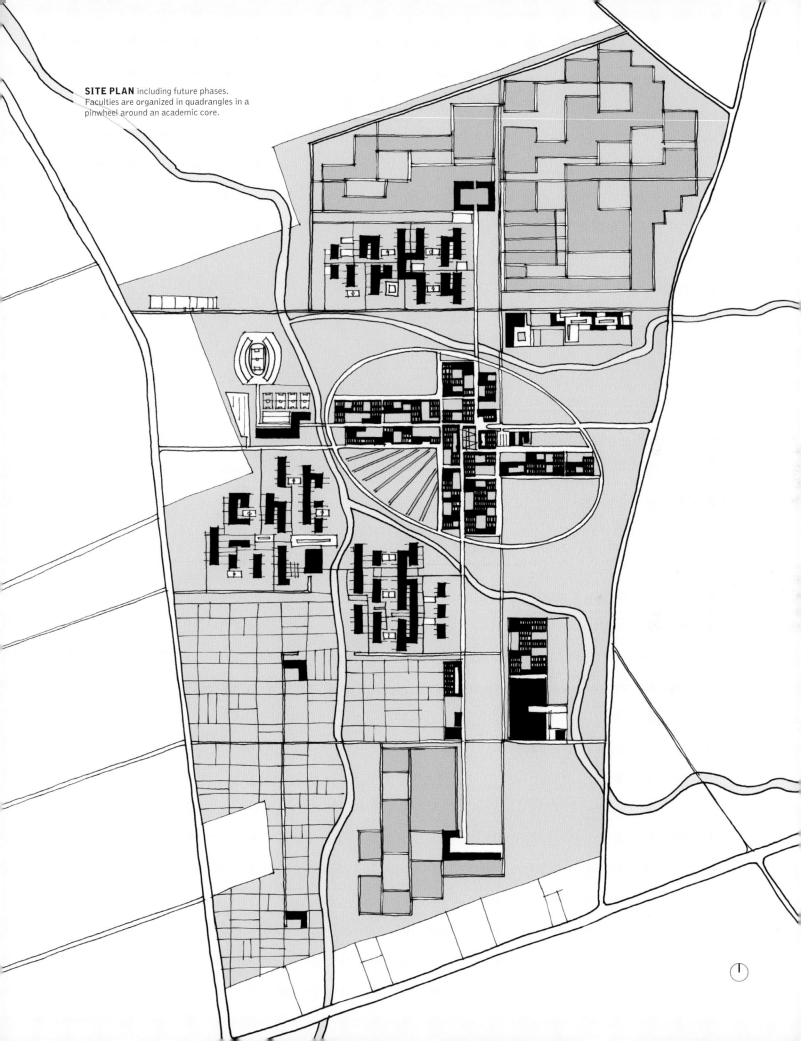

SITE PLAN including future phases.
Faculties are organized in quadrangles in a
pinwheel around an academic core.

MAIN LIBRARY The main library and its plaza act as the academic hub of the university.

SUSTAINABLE STRATEGIES The campus employs a range of natural cooling and shading strategies, such as overhanging louvred canopies.

UNDULATING ROOF CANOPY spans the classroom buildings and their courtyards. Its angles create pressure differentiation to maximize airflow.

TWO.SEVEN

TRANSNATIONAL EDUCATION

MASTER PLAN
YALE-NUS

Singapore 2011– 4 ha (10.5 acres)
Master planner: Pfeiffer Partners Architects/KieranTimberlake

DUBBED ONE OF THE FOUR 'ASIAN TIGERS', IN RECENT DECADES
SINGAPORE HAS EMERGED AS AN ECONOMIC POWERHOUSE. ONE
OF THE WORLD'S RICHEST NATIONS, IT HAS FUELLED ITS GROWTH
THROUGH A SUSTAINED INVESTMENT IN EDUCATION FOR THE
STEM DISCIPLINES.

THE COMMONS, CENTRAL COURT Colonnades
and overhanging roofs are used as protection from
the Singaporean sun and rain.

The National University of Singapore (NUS), accordingly, ranks amongst Asia's best research universities. A consequence of this approach, though, is that the humanities have been largely overlooked. A collaboration between NUS and the US's Yale University, however, seeks to counter this trend. Yale-NUS is Singapore's first liberal arts college, offering four-year undergraduate degrees across the arts, humanities, and social and natural sciences. It is being funded in full by the Singaporean government. Coming in tandem with other partnerships with MIT and Duke University's Medical School, its foundation is a reflection of the country's wider strategy to position itself as an education hub for Asia.

When the venture was first announced in 2011, controversy and scepticism was rife. Nevertheless, construction of a campus quickly began in July 2012 and completion is scheduled for 2015. The ethical and political debate that has accompanied the partnership is beyond the remit of this study; instead we focus attention on how this alliance is being translated in physical terms through its master plan. The plan was produced by Pfeiffer Partners Architects with KieranTimberlake, while Pelli Clarke Pelli Architects alongside Forum Architects are the design architects.

Located adjacent to NUS's main site, the campus has been shaped by a design philosophy of East meets West. Evoking the quadrangular organization of Yale's New Haven base, the plan uses the courtyard as a structural device. University life is focused upon a rectangular green bounded by teaching, administrative, and recreational buildings, including the learning commons, performance hall, and sports centre. In the Yale tradition of ceremonial gateways, the central green is accessed via a large covered entryway. This motif is given a tropical twist however; its roof is pierced with a square oculus, from which pours a theatrical cascade of rainwater into a circular reflecting pool below. The college's equatorial setting is further reflected in the colonnades and overhanging eaves that characterize its buildings. They offer protection from Singapore's extremes of sun and rain, while also visually uniting the ensemble of structures. Parity can be drawn with the regional tradition of the five-foot way, pedestrian walkways that are indented into the ground floors of buildings and are thereby sheltered by the overhanging upper storeys.

Arguably, the plan's biggest manifestation of its Singaporean context comes with its scale and density. To accommodate all functions on the modest plot, quadrangular organization is married with high-rise structures, specifically for Yale-NUS's three residential colleges. Dedicated student residences have not historically been part of Singaporean tertiary education. Nonetheless, from the early discussions a key attribute of the new institution has been its replication of Yale's signature college system. Containing all the expected ingredients of a residential house – dining halls, dormitories, classrooms, faculty offices – the colleges are arranged around individual courtyards and housed in tower blocks. In an attempt to humanize their scale and foster collegiality, each block is divided into 'neighbourhoods', grouped vertically around communal 'skygardens'. Positioned every third floor, the gardens provide semi-open patios heavily landscaped with plants capable of withstanding high-rise conditions. Native flora is set to play a significant role. The courtyards will have a plentiful tree canopy to provide extra shade, including six existing mature trees conserved in the campus green.

With this blend of tropical high rises and collegiate living, the master plan is seeking to invest the new university with a unique and instant identity. Upon a constrained site, it balances the disparate cultural, academic, and climatic influences of the two founding partners.

TROPICAL ENTRYWAY Access to the campus core is via a dramatic gateway complete with theatrical cascade of rainwater.

COLLEGIATE SYSTEM Three residential colleges are grouped around individual courtyards shaded by native planting.

MASTER PLAN
CORNELL TECH

New York, USA 2011– $2bn 5 ha (12.5 acres)
Master planner: Skidmore, Owings & Merrill

LATE IN 2010, MAYOR BLOOMBERG OF NEW YORK CITY LAUNCHED
A GLOBAL COMPETITION TO DEVELOP A NEW ENGINEERING AND
APPLIED SCIENCES CAMPUS IN MANHATTAN.

CAMPUS FOR THE NEXT CENTURY The
campus is a staging ground for Cornell Tech's unique
academic experiment.

This was to be a special type of institution. Unconventionally, the principal impetus for the initiative was not educational, but rather stemmed from the 2008 economic crash which had exposed the degree to which the city was dependent on the financial sector. After a year of lobbying, the winner was announced: a partnership of Cornell University and the Technion-Israel Institute of Technology, known as Cornell Tech. Cornell Tech is seen as a key driver in fuelling a start-up boom in New York City by harnessing the strengths of the Ivy League Cornell and the Haifa-based public research university dubbed the MIT of Israel. The new campus, for which construction commenced in 2014, has already been nicknamed Silicon Alley.

As part of the contest, Cornell Tech was awarded a 99-year lease, along with $100 million in city capital for infrastructure and maintenance, to a 5-hectare (12.5-acre) site on Roosevelt Island. This narrow strip of land – boasting scenic views but underutilized – lies in the middle of the East River adjacent to Manhattan. The master plan, developed by Skidmore, Owings & Merrill (SOM) and landscape architects James Corner Field Operations, envisions a campus of low-rise futuristic buildings zigzagging down a pedestrian spine (known as Techwalk) carefully aligned to capture vistas towards iconic points in the city skyline. 'Our campus won't look like any other university campus that exists today', the dean of Cornell Tech has boasted.[23]

The campus is planned to contain three academic buildings, three residential structures, three for research and development, plus a hotel and conference centre. The centrepiece is an academic building designed by Thom Mayne of Morphosis. This is to be no soaring skyscraper. A key design feature, also replicated by almost every other building on campus, is that it is limited in height to five storeys, or approximately the height of the deck of the Queensboro Bridge which passes over the island. Intended to encourage interaction and collaboration, the building's design places an emphasis on openness. A large atrium opens onto a grand staircase at the core of the structure, designated as a vertical circulation corridor that incorporates landings with meeting areas. Lifts have been pushed to the building's periphery to discourage use. Connectivity underpins the campus's ethos. A corporate colocation building for example will bring students side-by-side with entrepreneurs and technology industry professionals. Designed by Weiss/Manfredi, its collaborative ambitions are manifested in transparent hallways, a glazed atrium, common spaces, and open floor plans. The buildings themselves are connected by a network of open space. Reported

to be a persuasive factor in Cornell Tech's 2011 victory, the master plan allots a strong commitment to creating public open space. Over a hectare (2.5 acres) will be devoted to it and, to render it welcoming and accessible to all, there will be no gates or fences.

This liberal provision is part of a wider commitment to the environment. The master plan features a slew of energy-saving devices, including stormwater recovery, a 1.8MW solar energy system, and a 'deep earth' geothermal well field to provide heating, cooling, and also recharge fuel cells. By far the most striking feature of Mayne's academic building, which aspires to net-zero energy use, is its 'lily-pad' roof composed of 8,000 square metres (87,000 square feet) of solar panels. If phase one is completed in adherence with the original plan, the 37,000-square-metre (400,000-square-feet) plot will generate as much energy as it uses.

It is a bold, aspirational goal, but given Cornell Tech's raison d'être to inspire innovation and cutting-edge technology in the city, such ambitions are wholly apposite.

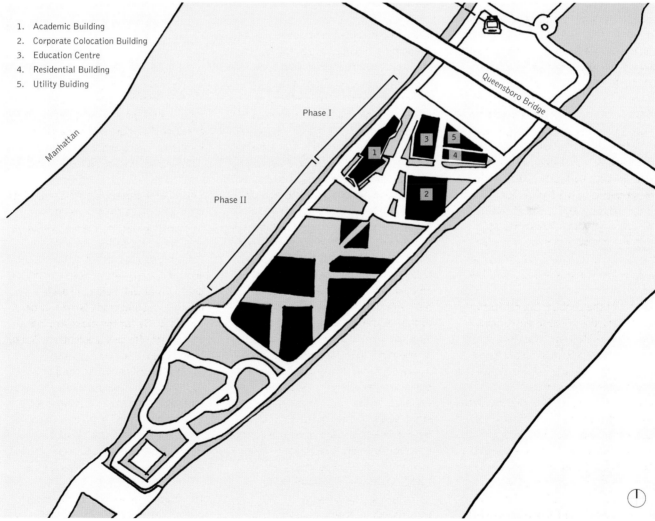

1. Academic Building
2. Corporate Colocation Building
3. Education Centre
4. Residential Building
5. Utility Buiding

Phase I

Phase II

Manhattan

Queensboro Bridge

AERIAL OF PHASE I No building will be taller than the deck of the Queensboro Bridge.

MASTER PLAN Buildings are linked by a north-south pedestrian spine, the Tech Walk.

CAMPUS PLAZA The completed campus will include over a hectare of open public space.

FUTURISTIC ARCHITECTURE 'Our campus won't look like any other university campus.'

FIRST PHASE BUILDINGS The first academic building (left), designed by Thom Mayne of Morphosis, has garnered media attention for its energy credentials.

MASTER PLAN
XI'AN JIAOTONG LIVERPOOL UNIVERSITY

Suzhou, China 2013 (Phase I) 16 ha (40 acres)
Master planner: Perkins+Will (Phase I)/BDP (Phase 2)

2013 SAW THE COMPLETION OF THE FIRST PHASE OF A
PIONEERING TRANSNATIONAL CAMPUS IN SUZHOU, ONE OF
CHINA'S MAJOR ECONOMIC ZONES, TO HOUSE THE XI'AN JIAOTONG
LIVERPOOL UNIVERSITY (XJTLU) – THE FIRST INDEPENDENT
SINO-FOREIGN UNIVERSITY.

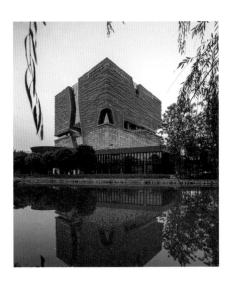

**ADMINISTRATION AND INFORMATION
BUILDING** The phase I building houses various
centres for learning, administration training, and
student activities.

China's strategy for higher education is on the fast track. With state spending on education annually increasing at approximately 22 per cent since 2008,[24] the nation's learning landscape is rapidly expanding. A key approach has been the forging of international links, notably with UK universities, carefully steered by the Chinese government. The University of Nottingham has operated a branch campus in Ningbo since 2004, while in Shanghai the Northern Group of UK universities offers degrees through the Sino-British College. As the country's first autonomous partnership institution, however, XJTLU breaks new ground. The collaborative venture unites the University of Liverpool, one of the UK's largest research-intensive institutions, with Xi'an Jiaotong University, a member of China's elite C9 group, building on a longstanding past relationship which has seen collaborative research stretching over some three decades. Jointly run and funded, the new university was officially inaugurated in 2006.

Located in the Dushu Lake Higher Education Town (HET) within Suzhou Industrial Park, the campus is set in what can be described as a 'ready-made' community of learning. Covering 1,000 hectares (2,500 acres), HET hosts 18 higher education organizations including Nanjing University, Southeast University, and Soochow University integrated within the wider framework of R&D industry and businesses. While

XJTLU benefits from HET's shared amenities such as sports centre, library, and restaurants, its establishment was marked by the construction of its own dedicated estate to house a total population of 10,000 students.

The master plan divides the 40-hectare (100-acre) site into North Campus (completed 2013) and South Campus (construction commenced 2013), which will be connected via a sunken underpass lined with retail units. Notwithstanding the venerable ancestry of the two partnering institutions, the venture aspires to create a new type of learning environ that fuses the traditions of East and West.

From the outset, the plan took its cues from the nearby Classical Gardens of Suzhou. Although now China's fourth largest urban economy, Suzhou is still celebrated for its ancient gardens. This heritage is translated into a plan that weaves buildings into a landscape of water pools, green walls, rooftop gardens, and shaded pedestrian pathways. The design lexicon is one of intimate ground-level courtyards and elevated green plazas. Completed buildings such as the vast four-wing Building 2 for science and research (Perkins and Will, 2010) demonstrate this through the synergetic flow between exterior spaces and interior classrooms, lecture theatres, and laboratories; notably, the green roof of the two-storey podium base which houses

the lecture theatres provides a spacious setting for casual socializing. Similarly, the Administration and Information Building (Aedas, 2013) is structured around a network of roof gardens, terraces, and an internal courtyard void which creates a naturally-lit stage for informal interaction.

The generous landscape provision responds to a key institutional goal to integrate spaces for both formal and informal learning. Reflecting Western pedagogic thinking, this approach considers the interaction that takes place outside the classroom as equal in importance in the academic experience to that occurring within. The heed allotted to connected, welcoming outdoor spaces is intended to support the promotion of cross-community communication and collaboration and thereby extend the learning environment across the campus. The close relationship between building and landscape as an environmental and pedagogic device is what distinguishes XJTLU's setting. Although essentially trading from the academic reputation of its two parent institutions, the new university has aimed to set itself apart from its progenitors by asserting its own physical identity in which building and nature – formal and informal space – harmoniously interact.

BUILDING 2 The vast, four-wing building for science and research is connected by a second-level circulation network.

BUILDING 2 The two-storey podium base is landscaped to provide informal external learning spaces.

PHASE 2 MASTER PLAN Construction of South Campus began in 2013 and is expected to last until 2015. It will connect to North Campus via an underground tunnel.

TWO.EIGHT

COMMERCIAL URBAN DEVELOPMENTS

EAST CAMPUS MALL
UNIVERSITY OF WISCONSIN–MADISON

Wisconsin, USA 2005– $500m 7 city blocks
Master planner: Consortium including SmithGroupJJR

WITH A STUDENT POPULATION IN THE REGION OF 42,000, THE
UNIVERSITY OF WISCONSIN–MADISON IS RANKED AS A TOP-TIER
STATE UNIVERSITY WHILE MADISON ITSELF IS REGARDED AS
ONE OF AMERICA'S GREAT COLLEGE TOWNS.

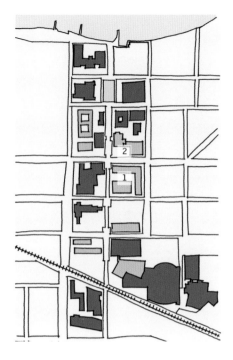

EAST CAMPUS MALL PLAN The phased
regeneration project has included University Square
(1) and an expansion of the Chazen Museum (2).

Historically, the centre of gravity for student life has been to the east of campus, which is linked to downtown via State Street, a vibrant mostly-pedestrianized thoroughfare. The East Campus Mall, however, seeks to create a new gateway between the city and university to the south of campus, an area that has habitually had an underused, redundant character. Its mix of proprietorship – university- and privately-owned land – had historically contributed to difficulties in effecting unified, comprehensive development. The Mall is a fifteen-year, cooperative programme funded in part by a private-public partnership.

The East Campus Mall was first proposed over 100 years ago within the university's 1909 Beaux-Arts master plan. Its suggestion for a pedestrian walkway at the northeast end of campus was never implemented, but in 1998 the idea was revived and revised. The venture is creating a seven-block, mixed-use pedestrian corridor that both acts as a new gateway to campus and connects it to retail, rental accommodation, and student services. The first stage of the scheme saw the realization of University Square in 2008, a 1.4-hectare (3.4-acre) plot comprising a nine-storey student services block and 12-storey apartment tower with underground parking and retail which replaced a 1970s strip mall. A second phase, concluded in 2012, saw a new academic building, museum expansion,

café, landscaping, and public art, while the final phase will see the delivery of a series of related projects known as the Lakefront Gateway, which embraces the university's setting on Lake Mendota by opening up the view from the south end of campus to the lake.

When fully realized, the project will have transformed 227,000 square metres (2,450,000 square feet) of low-density brownfield into cultural, retail, academic, and residential space that blends into the surrounding city. The portion already completed has delivered an urban experience, with ground-floor shops along a pedestrianized street and hardscaped plaza. The plaza – University Square – is the cornerstone of the East Campus Mall. The largest infill project ever built in Madison, it covers an entire city block and has added richness and density to an underutilized parcel of land. Its offering of rental accommodation for students and young professionals, in particular, has proven a popular component of the scheme. It is credited with having spurred private apartment developments nearby, as symptomatic of the changes that the Mall is bringing upon the character of the neighbourhood.

While the retail is generally student-oriented, including a bike shop, a yoga studio, and a salon, the wider community has also embraced it; on a summer evening, the area is populated by cyclists, joggers, and pedestrians from college

age upwards. Improvements to the old infrastructure have been as important in achieving this success as the new buildings. The junction adjacent to University Square where the mall meets University Avenue – one of the city's widest and busiest streets – has been given special paving treatment to emphasize the continuity of the Mall. Such devices are vital for both place-making and safety. The Mall's importance as a campus thoroughfare is highlighted by the fact that it has become a popular parking spot for an informal campus bike-sharing scheme, and it is common to see students picking up or dropping off bikes.

The eastern edge of campus had long been an underperforming, disorderly area. The East Campus Mall can be lauded as a successful fusion of university-city cooperation, drawing together multiple landowners to create a mixed-use precinct serving both university members and Madison at large.

NEW FRONT DOOR The mall is a gateway between the city and campus. View southwards towards Chazen Museum addition.

UNIVERSITY SQUARE A university-private partnership containing student services, rental apartments, and retail.

PEDESTRIAN CORRIDOR The mixture of landscape, retail, housing, cultural, and university facilities adds density and activity to an underutilized area.

NORTH WEST CAMBRIDGE

Cambridge, UK 2012– £1bn 150 ha (370 acres)
Master planner: AECOM

PHASE 1 Ground breaking on site commenced in 2013 and construction is expected to span a 20-year timeframe.

THE UNIVERSITY OF CAMBRIDGE, ONE OF THE OLDEST IN THE WORLD, ROUTINELY VIES FOR THE TOP SPOT ON INTERNATIONAL RANKING TABLES.

Even so, it cannot rest on its laurels and within the current competitive environment is constantly working to maintain its world-class calibre. 'The greatest contribution that the handful of the world's leading universities can make,' asserted the Vice-Chancellor in a 2012 speech, 'is to strive to remain in that handful: the constant competition of the top few global universities keeps the leading edge sharp.'[25] Early in the 2000s plans were set in motion to safeguard this long-term position with a vast, £1 billion expansion, the largest in the university's 800-year history, on 150 hectares (370 acres) of university-owned farmland northwest of the city centre.

The development arose from two pressing demands: firstly, the lack of affordable accommodation; Cambridge is already one of the UK's most constrained housing markets and the university estimated that in the next 20 years it will add 3,000 staff and 5,000 student places. Secondly, the continued necessity to expand its research profile and foster links between business and academic interests that have already given the area a reputation as 'Silicon Fen'. The university is prioritizing postgraduate and postdoctoral researchers as its prime channel for future growth to sustain its reputation for research excellence. To attract the best students and staff, relieving the acute

shortage of economical housing is imperative, as is providing modern research and incubator space. North West Cambridge will include 100,000 square metres (1,000,000 square feet) of academic and R&D space, up to 1,500 subsidized homes for staff, and accommodation for 2,000 postgraduates.

However, while the impetus for the project was to serve the long-term academic and research goals of the university, it has evolved into an urban venture much larger in its ambitions. Part urban extension, part living-learning community, North West Cambridge will be a new neighbourhood unto itself, comprising retail, primary school, GP surgery, nursery, and up to 1,500 houses for private sale.

Ground-breaking on site commenced in 2013, after a ten-year master planning and consultation process. While the overall master plan has been authored by AECOM, a range of architectural practices are responsible for individual tracts. The selection of architects for phase one, which includes Stirling Prize-winning practices such as Stanton Williams, Wilkinson Eyre, and Alison Brooks, provides a telling indication of the superior quality of environment to which the university is aspiring. The university has repeatedly voiced its commitment to high-

standard architecture, landscape, and placemaking. Central to this is the master plan's open space provision – 60 hectares (150 acres) acres in total. The plan utilizes the existing network of hedgerows, ditches, and trees, and, in tune with the bike-friendly ethos of the city centre, incorporates an extensive nexus of cycle routes and 11,500 cycle parking spaces.

The entire site has been devised to minimize the need for private cars, with its planners estimating that only 30 per cent of commuters to the site will be single-occupancy vehicles. Sustainable design and living is a priority of the scheme. Its environmental credentials boast zero-carbon housing and stormwater recharge. Notwithstanding that the land was removed from the greenbelt to enable its development, North West Cambridge has elicited relatively modest local opposition. Critiques centre upon fears of 'a separate university enclave'.[26] The university intends to offer its key worker housing to staff at below-market rents, while it will also control sports pitches

PHASE I LOCAL CENTRE Comprising public plaza, supermarket, retail, and post-doctoral accommodation.

POST-GRADUATE STUDENT ACCOMMODATION
Designed by RH Partnership.

---

and allotments. In counterbalance, though, the community centre and central open space will be administered in partnership with the city council, and the first phase comprises local facilities such as shops, school, and supermarket, and over 400 market homes.

With the construction forecast to occupy 20 years, the scale of the undertaking will have a significant impact upon both the region and university. Since its foundation in the thirteenth century, the institution has always had a deep-rooted symbiosis with its host city. The scope of North West Cambridge, nevertheless, is a telling bellwether of the role of higher education institutions in transforming city frameworks.

AERIAL RENDERING The mixed-use development will transform 150 hectares of farmland into residential, academic and research facilities, and public amenities.

DISCOVERY RISE
JAMES COOK UNIVERSITY

Queensland, Australia 2010– Aus$1.3bn 60 ha (150 acres)
Master planner: Architectus

CONSTRUCTED IN THE 1960S, THE DOUGLAS CAMPUS OF JAMES COOK UNIVERSITY (JCU) TYPIFIES THE DESIGN MORES OF THE TIME. BUILT ON GREENFIELD LAND 13 KILOMETRES (8 MILES) OUTSIDE CENTRAL TOWNSVILLE IN QUEENSLAND, IT GREW AS A SPRAWLING, CAR-DEPENDENT SITE.

COURTYARD HOUSES Discovery Village's housing embraces low-energy design features to suit Townsville's dry tropical climate such as shallow building plans, breezeways, and louvres.

While the area surrounding the university has since progressively urbanized and is forecast to grow substantially in forthcoming decades, the campus itself has remained suburban, detached from the city, and at odds with JCU's aspirations towards sustainability. The launch of Discovery Rise in 2008 sought to remedy this.

This is a pioneering development by JCU, intended as a testing ground for the creation of a unique urbanism appropriate to Townsville's tropical context. The aim of the project is to recast and remodel the campus's physical environment from an isolated, institutional estate into Discovery Rise, a miniature university town seamlessly integrated with Townsville. It is, in effect, a total campus retrofit. Over a two-decade timespan, the campus core will be rejuvenated and vacant land at the edge of campus will be utilized to create a mixed-use academic, residential, and commercial community housing up to 8,000 residents.

The master plan is divided into a series of five connected but distinct villages created within existing sites and built anew upon open land west and south of the academic core. These five villages are: the DR Enterprise Park, a research commercial quarter for education, health, and defence-sector businesses; University Central, hosting university-orientated facilities such as student housing and academic buildings; the Discovery Community Precinct, a mixed-density community with primary

and secondary schools, sports facilities, and a range of family and retiree homes; Discovery Rise Village, a medium-density, child-friendly residential community; and Discovery Central, a vibrant town centre branded as the meeting ground of 'Town and Gown'. Discovery Central was the first part of the scheme to be commenced beginning with the Clinical Practice Building (2013), a five-storey teaching facility including dentistry, pharmacy, psychiatry, and physiotherapy that is open to the community and includes ground-floor retail. Discovery Central will breathe new life into the historic campus core, by densifying the site through infill development. It will combine social, commercial, residential, and education facilities centred upon a new public square, the Ideas Market.

Each of the five precincts are connected by pedestrian-friendly streets and lanes lined with trees, verandas, shaded parks, and public spaces. JCU is actively seeking to overhaul its suburban character to become a world leader in developing urban sustainability. Discovery Rise's walkability is essential to this. The master plan's layering of planting, colonnades, and verandas provides a continuous network of shelter to encourage pedestrian life in the hot and humid climate. Narrow, east-west thoroughfares, where thermal mass and shade keeps streets cool, are combined with north-south roads with large-scale planted cover and built shade at intersections.

In many aspects, the master plan has been conditioned by JCU's ambitions towards sustainability and the campus's location in the parkland tropics of northern Queensland. The retention of mature trees and enhancement of natural waterways has figured large within the design, as have ecological initiatives such as green walls and roofs and self-contained energy systems. The tropical backdrop has inspired the colours and materials of the landscape and architecture. Furthermore, additional public transport options between campus and downtown Townsville are being instigated to discourage car use.

Although still at an early stage, Discovery Rise has the promise to spearhead a new approach to campus urbanism within this environmentally-conscious age. Like many Australian universities, JCU was purpose-built in the 1960s on a vast tract of greenfield land. Fifty years later, this generation of institutions is finding that its campus edge has changed, as have the needs and wants of students. In making an attempt to move from a suburban to an urban environment, JCU is potentially creating a roadmap for other universities of the same vintage to reimagine their campuses for an increasingly competitive and multifarious age.

DISCOVERY CENTRAL JCU's town centre will be pedestrian orientated and include retail, housing, offices, and university buildings.

MASTER PLAN Discovery Rise is divided into five villages. When fully developed, it is anticipated to house 8,000 people.

Proposed New Development

Existing Development

Future Investigation Area

COURTYARD APARTMENTS Discovery Village will contain a mix of market housing types: apartments, townhouses, and small detached dwellings.

COURTYARD APARTMENTS SECTION Semi-private courtyards, shared garden terraces, and private verandas characterize their design.

THE IDEAS MARKET At the heart of Discovery Central will be a covered 'souk' surrounded by housing, offices, and JCU facilities on upper levels and shops and cafés at ground level.

TWO.NINE

LARGE-SCALE
CAMPUS
EXPANSIONS

GREATER BELFAST DEVELOPMENT
UNIVERSITY OF ULSTER–BELFAST

Belfast, UK 2012– £250m 8,400m² (90,000ft²)
Master planner: Feilden Clegg Bradley Studios

FOR MANY UNIVERSITIES, THE 2008 ECONOMIC CRASH
TRIGGERED A STRING OF CHALLENGES. THE UNIVERSITY OF
ULSTER, HOWEVER, SAW IN IT AN OPPORTUNITY.

ENTRANCE FOYER Large, double-height atria
bring natural light deep into the building plan.

The university has capitalized on the property slump in Belfast by buying up a number of properties adjacent to its city-centre campus that it otherwise would not have had the chance to acquire. In February 2012, it announced plans to demolish many of its new acquisitions and expand its Belfast campus by building in their stead three mid-rise buildings, two connected via a sky bridge. The new construction will allow the university to relocate students and staff from the suburban Jordanstown campus several miles away. The effect will be a vibrant, dense urban campus that will boost the university's operational and academic efficiencies through the consolidation of its activities. The expanded Belfast campus will house the institution's 15,000 students in £250 million of new facilities, totalling approximately 75,000 square metres (800,000 square feet).

The university hopes that the boons from the expansion will not just be of benefit to itself. It anticipates that a modernized campus and greater student density will bring about neighbourhood revitalization to an area that has been hard-hit by the economic recession. Administrators aspire that the new campus will help widen access to higher education and provide a new, improved platform from which the institution can engage communities. Consolidating the campus in an urban rather than suburban area was part of its goal to become more inclusive.

Feilden Clegg Bradley Studios, a Stirling Prize-winning practice, designed the three buildings for the new campus. Neighbouring the existing architecture school, they provide space for faculties of computing and engineering, life sciences, social sciences, business, and arts. Their design, Feilden Clegg Bradley has explained, takes its inspiration from dual sources: the topography of Northern Ireland, and the need to be sensitive to the site context. In the first instance, the buildings have a clear base, middle, and top, taken from the geological stratification of the landscape. In the second, they respond to the mixed urban context of the Cathedral Quarter, where the University of Ulster is located. To the south, the campus is bounded by nineteenth-century conservation areas; to the north, by commercial and residential areas. The university's new buildings range in height from four to twelve storeys to reflect the changing cityscape across the site and knit the large scheme into Belfast's historic fabric.

Given its urban realm, the new campus is permeable to city residents and has been designed to sit seamlessly within Belfast. The three lower floors of the expanded campus will be accessible to the public, and the university seeks to achieve a similar permeability across faculties and disciplines.

The three buildings are organized in a triangle around an intersection at the centre of campus, creating a centre of gravity for students and a new entryway and degree of visibility for the university. The largest of the buildings will act as a new gateway to the campus. Termed the 'lantern' building, it includes a flatiron tower with glazed floor-to-ceiling windows. Glass windows across upper floors of all three buildings will allow passers-by unusual sightlines into the academic space, blurring the boundaries between the academic and urban realms. The interior will have a similar degree of porosity; all the buildings will have double-height atria, cantilevered spaces on the upper floors, and bridges that will emphasize the openness of the space. Seen from afar, the campus will be both architecturally imposing and visually porous.

Construction began in 2013. When completed in 2018, the scheme is poised to usher in a new chapter in the university's academic life and its relationship with the city.

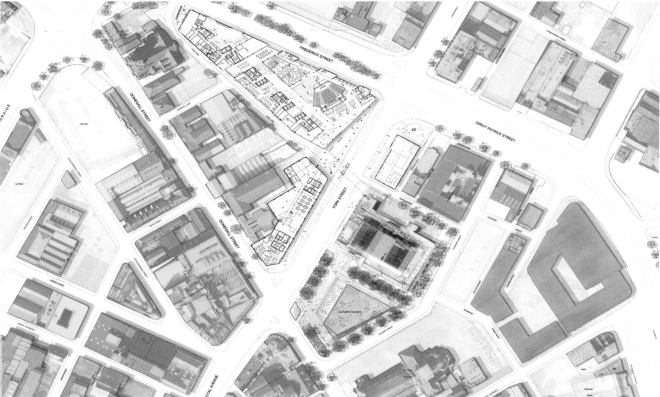

YORK STREET ELEVATION The new buildings
utilize a palette of brick and glass.

SITE PLAN The development comprises three large
buildings housing six faculties.

ENTRANCE FOYER Double-height atria, cantilevered
levels, and glazed walls characterize the interior.

YORK STREET ENTRANCE An 'air bridge'
connects to an adjacent building within the scheme.

MANHATTANVILLE COLUMBIA UNIVERSITY

New York, USA 2011– $6.3bn 6.8 ha (17 acres)
Master planner: Renzo Piano Building Workshop/Skidmore, Owings and Merrill

MANHATTAN'S COLUMBIA UNIVERSITY IS FAMED FOR ITS INTIMATE BEAUX ARTS CAMPUS IN MORNINGSIDE HEIGHTS DESIGNED IN THE 1890s. ALTHOUGH ORIGINALLY BUILT ON FARMLAND, TODAY IT IS IN ALL RESPECTS AN URBAN CAMPUS ENCIRCLED BY ONE OF THE WORLD'S MOST EFFERVESCENT METROPOLISES.

JEROME L. GREEN SCIENCE CENTRE
The first of Manhattanville's buildings, due for completion in 2016.

This prime location, however, has brought its challenges, most notably when it comes to expanding its facilities to keep pace with peer institutions. While the university has continually grown within the envelope of its 1897 master plan, it has also looked for expansion opportunities beyond its immediate confines; both its medical and athletic facilities are located several miles north of the historic campus. Its current expansion plan, though, exceeds anything contemplated before, in size, scope, and complexity.

In 2003, the university unveiled plans for a new campus, christened Manhattanville. Scheduled for completion in 2030, the 7-hectare (17-acre) site begins half a mile north of the present estate and, at build-out, will include 15 new buildings housing teaching, research, and support services set within a network of open space. Construction on the first of these, the 42,000-square-metre (450,000-square-foot) Jerome L. Green Science Centre, began in 2013 and is projected to continue until 2016.

The master plan marks a distinct departure from the Morningside Heights prototype. Whereas the campus's perimeter of tall red-brick buildings with high granite bases consciously created an academic citadel, Manhattanville is imagined as a place of transparency and urbanity.

Respecting the existing street grid, its plan uses city blocks to structure the campus. Streets will remain open to public traffic, ground-floor space will house retail and community uses, pavements will be widened to encourage pedestrian life, and façades will be largely glazed. One of the most remarked-upon features of the plan is its network of subterranean service roads hidden within a contiguous basement, obviating the need for surface-level deliveries and utilities and creating a near-unbroken line of street-level activity.

This underground infrastructure is an essential mechanism in delivering the master plan's generous provision of open space accessible to all. Notwithstanding the difficulties of achieving new green space in a crowded urban context, especially one as dense as Manhattan, the scheme is set to incorporate nearly a hectare (over two acres) of it. A large public square will provide an outdoor setting for collegiate and community events, while a significant tree-planting programme is scheduled.

However, in spite of the plan's emphasis on permeability and accessibility for the local community, heated opposition has dogged the scheme. Given its large scale and location, this is unsurprising. With all but four of the existing structures on the site being bulldozed, residents, business owners,

and community boards have expressed fears of displacement, gentrification, and job losses. Much of the antagonism has stemmed from Columbia's divisive use of eminent domain (compulsory purchase) in acquiring the necessary land. Condemned by many as an act of belligerence, the acquisition was challenged by several landowners resulting in legal battles that scaled the state's courtrooms. By the time the project was unveiled, though, all but 12 per cent of the required area was already owned by the university, the state, and state-owned utility companies. Tensions still remain, but the university has promised a range of assuaging measures that has tempered some of the hostility. More than $20 million has been allotted to support affordable housing initiatives, plus an additional $76 million is being invested in community projects.

For Columbia, expansion was never going to be easy. The Manhattanville project takes the university into a contested neighbourhood realm. Yet its realization will see, if successful, a physical interlacing of academic and urban functions that has the potential to be an influential model for twenty-first-century campus creation.

AN URBAN CAMPUS Generous public realm and glazed ground-floor retail will draw urban life into Manhattanville.

PHASE I FROM BROADWAY New trees will be planted on Broadway and along cross streets.

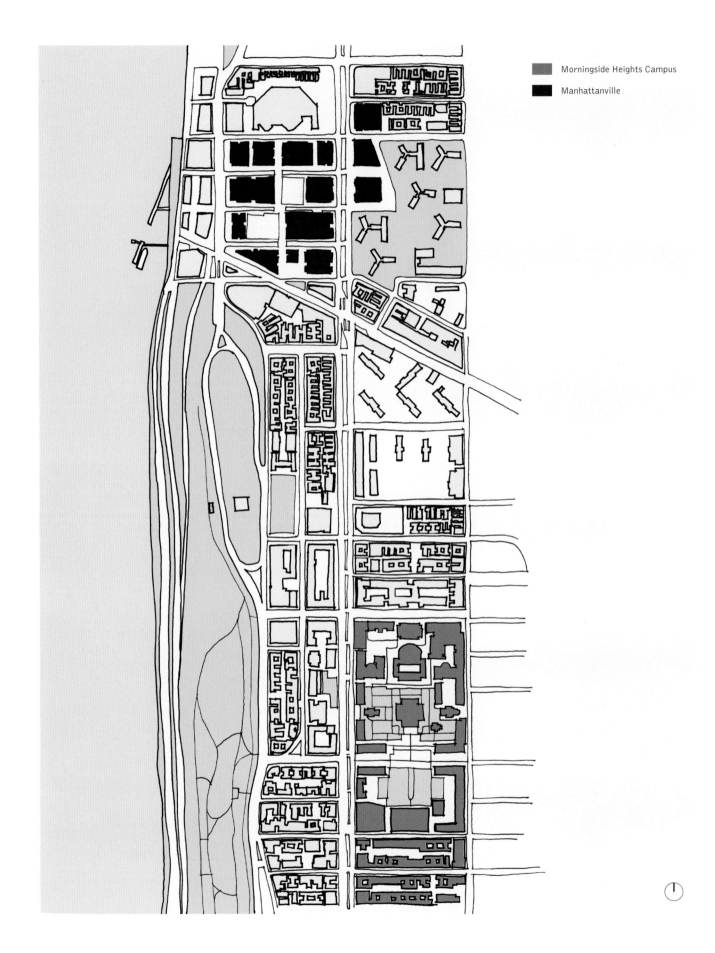

JEROME L. GREEN SCIENCE CENTRE
West façade. Designed by the Renzo Piano
Building Workshop, the sleek glassy building
will set the tone for the campus.

Opposite:
SITE PLAN Situated just north of Columbia's
present campus, Manhattanville is set for
completion in 2030.

IMPERIAL WEST
IMPERIAL COLLEGE LONDON

London, UK 2011– $1bn 10 ha (25 acres)
Master planner: Aukett Fitzroy Robinson

IN RECENT YEARS, IMPERIAL COLLEGE LONDON HAS INVESTED SIGNIFICANTLY IN ITS CAMPUS INFRASTRUCTURE. ALONGSIDE OTHER PARTNERS, IT HAS RESHAPED THE PEDESTRIAN REALM AROUND ITS SOUTH KENSINGTON CORE SITE TO CREATE A MORE CAMPUS-LIKE FEEL AND GIVE ENHANCED PROMINENCE TO ITS RESEARCH FACILITIES.

TECHNOLOGY TRANSFER BUILDING viewed from public square. Scheduled to house the largest concentration of affordable, flexible laboratory and office space in London.

Imperial West, however, represents a capital project on a much more ambitious scale. Determined to combat its space constraints on its central South Kensington base, in 2009 the college purchased two large parcels of land in an area of west London known as White City close to its Hammersmith hospital campus, on a plot formerly occupied by the BBC. The site was envisioned as the home of Imperial's largest expansion to date, creating a whole new campus christened Imperial West.

Designed by Aukett Fitzroy Robinson, Imperial West replicates the urbanity of the college's original campus with a modern architectural palette. It is not intended to be an academia-only realm, but is planned to encompass shops and open space shared by students and local residents that will bring jobs and a mixed-use vivacity to White City, a target of regional regeneration in itself. Imperial West's first buildings are already open. Completed in 2012, these are a series of student residences developed in partnership with a private developer housing 600 postgraduate students and young researchers. The campus will also include research buildings (one of which has received major capital donations from the Research Partnership Investment Fund and from Imperial's development partner Voreda Capital), leisure and retail facilities, a medical clinic, a nursery, market homes, and a large publicly-accessible square.

Like many expansions of this scale, the project has not been without controversy. This has focused upon the central landmark of the scheme, a glazed residential tower. At 35 storeys, it will be substantially taller than any other building in the vicinity. This scale has attracted fierce vitriol from local residents, earning itself its own nickname – the Imperial Folly – and its own website. Many neighbourhood groups are concerned about setting a precedent for the rapid urbanization of their neighbourhood.

However, to Imperial the expansion is perceived as an essential means of boosting its status as a catalyst of scientific discovery and economic growth on an international level. 'Our plans are to develop a campus for innovation at a scale we could not possibly do [on our South Kensington site] and make that a hub for collaboration and developing ideas to market on a scale that has not been seen in Europe before,' Professor David Gann, vice-president for innovation and development, has explained.[27] Its co-location of research, business, and healthcare will make Imperial West a first for the UK. The college has actively invited industry, the National Health Service, and academic partners to the campus to create what it calls an 'ecosystem' for education, research, translation, and commercialization. Its debt to US models is clear, notably the University of California San Francisco's Mission Bay and MIT's Kendall Square, where underutilized brownfield sites were developed to house interdisciplinary research facilities, university spin-offs, and multinational companies. The first phase of construction includes a Technology Transfer Building (designed by PLP Architecture), to house Imperial Innovations, the group responsible for the commercial development of the college's research endeavours. The building, composed of two wings seven- and twelve-floors tall, is intended to be as flexible as possible to provide laboratory, office, and research space that can be reconfigured to meet user demands over the coming decades. It is due to be completed in early 2015, with two further academic buildings following soon after. However, the complexity of the financial arrangements being used for the campus as a whole means that its realization is being spread over several stages and thus it will be the 2020s before Imperial West is functioning to its anticipated potential.

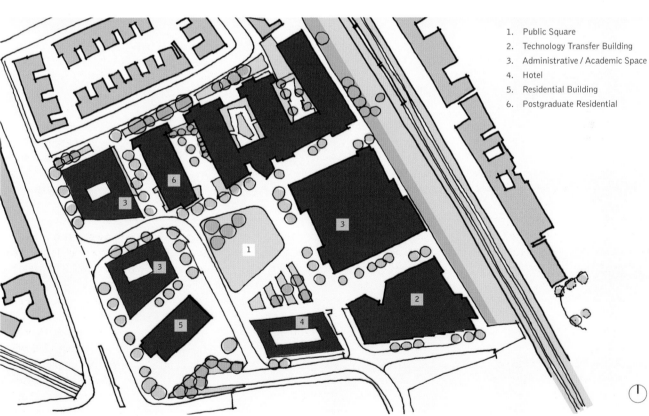

1. Public Square
2. Technology Transfer Building
3. Administrative / Academic Space
4. Hotel
5. Residential Building
6. Postgraduate Residential

PUBLICLY ACCESSIBLE Imperial West will be open to all, with community open space, fitness facilities, health centre, restaurants, and retail.

SITE PLAN The 25-acre site has been master planned by London-based practice Auckett Fitzroy Robinson.

CENTRAL PUBLIC SQUARE The one-acre open square is a campus focus. On the right is the controversial 35-storey residential tower containing 192 units.

TWO.TEN

REVITALIZING MASTER PLANS

MASTER PLAN
UNIVERSITY OF TEXAS AT AUSTIN

Texas, USA 2012– 175 ha (430 acres)
Master planner: Sasaki Associates

THE UNIVERSITY OF TEXAS AT AUSTIN HAS A LONG HISTORY OF
CAMPUS PLANNING. IT HAS NOW BEGUN A NEW CHAPTER IN THIS
STORY BY COMMISSIONING SASAKI ASSOCIATES TO GUIDE THE
IMMEDIATE AND LONG-RANGE GROWTH OF ITS CAMPUS.

MASTER PLANNING HERITAGE The
University's long history of master planning has
resulted in a dense campus core with a collection
of history buildings.

Since the college was founded on a 16-hectare (40-acre) site in 1883, its physical environment has been shaped largely during four stages of evolution: early development up to 1930, defined by the Beaux-Arts plan of Cass Gilbert (1910); the Paul Cret plan (1933), which established a strong organization of axes and courtyards; the Modernist era (1945–75), which saw enormous growth into the adjacent city grid; and the Post-Modern era and Cesar Pelli & Associates plan (1999), in which the pace of campus expansion slowed followed by a emphasis on re-creating a 'sense of community'. The result of this trajectory of master planning is one of the densest, and most iconic campus settings in the US with strong formal and visual relationships between landmarks, other buildings, and open spaces.

Sasaki's plan was unveiled in 2012. Significant development has occurred since the implementation of the Pelli plan, yet the university is now faced with new financial and strategic issues not envisaged in the 1990s. Sasaki's framework is purposed to guide development for the next decade and beyond to address the current climate. It identifies six principal tasks: an historical inventory and preservation plan; mobility plan; sustainability plan; space management tool; development framework plan; and design guidelines for buildings. It applies these to two focus areas of campus: Core campus and Central campus.[28] The 80 hectares (196 acres) of Core campus is a tightly-organized precinct containing the university's most celebrated buildings and vistas. Central campus (74 hectares, 182 acres), on the other hand, is much more suburban in character, less densely and formally developed. It is its recommendations for this latter, more challenging area of the estate that form the most thought-provoking and potentially-transformative aspect of the new master plan.

With far fewer buildings and trees than the Core, characterized instead by vast surface car parks and wide streets, Central campus suffers from its disparate layout, poor connectivity, and an unwelcoming pedestrian environment. The plan proposes to revitalize this precinct into a vibrant extension of the Core, remodelling its suburban character by introducing enhanced circulation networks, increased density, and improved building placement that fosters the development of the public realm.

Key to this strategy is the remodelling of the East Transit Mall – the prime means of connection between Core and Central campuses. What has hitherto been a barren road dominated by buses and traffic, Sasaki propose reshaping into a tree-lined, pedestrian-orientated thoroughfare lined with community and student facilities. The plan envisages that the street will be narrowed, creating space for wide, shaded walkways. New buildings with ground-level retail and services will face the mall, creating a well-defined and lively space.

With a similar goal of bringing more pedestrian life to Central campus, another recommendation of the plan is the creation of a new quadrangle directly north of the East Transit Mall and framed by the existing Visual Arts Centre and Fine Arts Building. It exemplifies the master plan's strategy of re-envisioning the outside spaces as landscape 'rooms'. Extending from the new quadrangle, a tree-lined promenade is planned which would provide a connection from the East Transit Mall to the northern edge of the Central zone. This framework of promenades and quadrangles deliberately responds to the planning traditions of the Core, reflecting the objective of translating the traditions of the historic campus as the university expands over the short and long term.

AERIAL LOOKING SOUTH The Core Campus's tight, quadrangular organization is used as a model for revitalizing Central Campus.

CENTRAL CAMPUS Sasaki's recommendations for Central Campus are the most transformative and potentially beneficial aspect of the new master plan.

THE MASTER PLAN Approved in 2013, the master plan will guide the growth of the University's three campus districts for the next 10 to 15 years.

CORE

W 27TH ST

E. DEAN KEETON ST

SAN JACINTO BLVD

SPEEDWAY

W 24TH ST

W 21ST ST

Future Building Opportunities

Existing Buildings

UT Austin Main Campus Boundary

W. MARTIN LUTHER KING JR BLVD

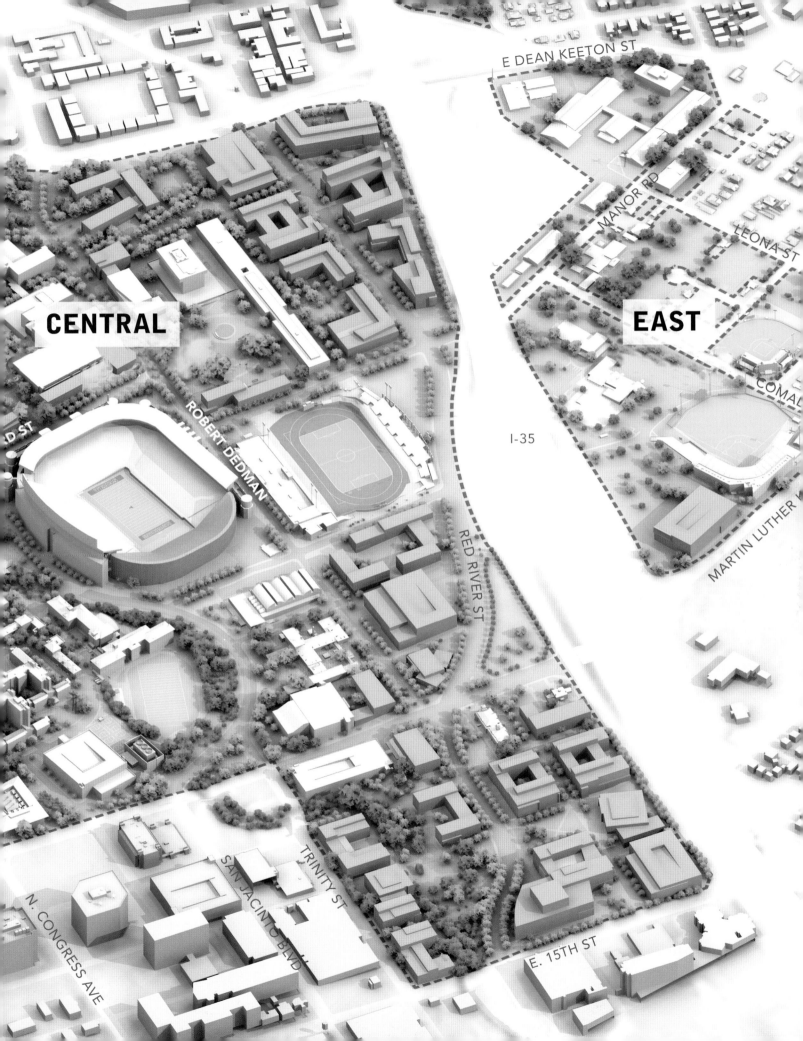

CENTRAL

EAST

E DEAN KEETON ST

MANOR RD

LEONA ST

ROBERT DEDMAN

I-35

RED RIVER ST

COMAL

MARTIN LUTHER

N. CONGRESS AVE

SAN JACINTO BLVD

TRINITY ST

E. 15TH ST

D ST

SCIENCE HILL PLAN
YALE UNIVERSITY

Connecticut, USA 1999– 11 ha (27 acres)
Master planner: Hillier Group/OLIN

CONSISTENTLY RANKED AMONGST THE WORLD'S TOP
UNIVERSITIES, YALE UNIVERSITY HAS A STRONG CONCERN WITH
STAYING AT THE FOREFRONT OF SCIENCE AND TECHNOLOGY.

INVITING LANDSCAPES The Science Hill
Plan has resulted in new, welcoming open
spaces, such as the quadrangle above adjoining
Kroon Hall.

The Science Hill precinct of its New Haven campus comprises various facilities primarily related to these disciplines. The land was purchased in 1910 and, like many science districts, has ever since been developed piece by piece.

Throughout its 300-year history, Yale's campus has been praised for the quality of its tight, urban landscape of quadrangles built in an eclectic mix of architectural styles, often by high-profile designers with great attention to detail. Science Hill, however, makes for a striking anomaly. Located outside the core campus, its ad hoc development together with the steep topography of the terrain has resulted in an ill-defined and neglected setting. It is characterized by a melange of paving styles, street furniture, and signage. Surface car parks and service areas scattered across the site only exaggerate its lack of order and block views towards the campus heart. Pedestrian connections between buildings and open spaces are haphazard and few. The open spaces themselves – several of which are large and prominently sited – are unwelcoming, not designed for any social use. The outcome is a lack of sense of place.

In the mid-1990s, Yale decided to take this matter in hand. In 1999 it unveiled a campus-wide master plan. The following year, as part of efforts to double the footprint of its science facilities over 20 years in line with institutional goals, it launched a specific Science Hill Plan by the Hillier Group. Its foci were threefold. Firstly, it made provision for new buildings and substantial retrofit projects, although several of these have fallen victim to the recession;[29] secondly, it sought to improve the landscape setting; and lastly, it addressed Science Hill's poor physical and social connections to the other parts of Yale's campus as well as to the wider city context. Landscape architects, OLIN, prepared a long-range open space plan to support the two latter ambitions. At the heart of this was a mission to radically enhance place-making, way-finding, pedestrian connections, and sense of importance of this vital part of the Yale estate. Intended to guide the growth of the Science Hill landscape for the following four decades, OLIN's plan sought to relink and rebuild Science Hill into a coherent and functional landscape based upon a layout of interconnected courtyards and quadrangles framed by new and existing buildings.

The plan aimed to take Science Hill's challenging topography and use it to its advantage. Teaching and research were grouped atop the hill and the intensive supporting services were located at a lower level, beneath the buildings. Service entrances were covered with new green areas to make it more people-friendly and aesthetically pleasing, while at the base of the hill, a welcoming entrance open space was proposed.

The enaction of the Science Hill Plan is on-going, but its recommendations are progressively being instigated. In 2009, the completion of Kroon Hall for the School of Forestry and Environmental Studies saw the creation of two new quadrangular landscapes between the neo-gothic Osborn Memorial Laboratory and Sage Bowers Hall, thus echoing the urban collegiate structure that dominates Yale's core campus. Appropriately enough for a faculty of Environmental Studies, the southern courtyard is a ground-level green roof built atop loading docks and utilities. Large-scale building renovations are also transforming the student and faculty experience. 2012 saw completion of the first phase of this remodelling.

Funding remains a problem for the continued development of Science Hill. However, the master plan is gradually being implemented as Yale delves deep in its pockets to ensure its position at the forefront of scientific research in the decades to come.

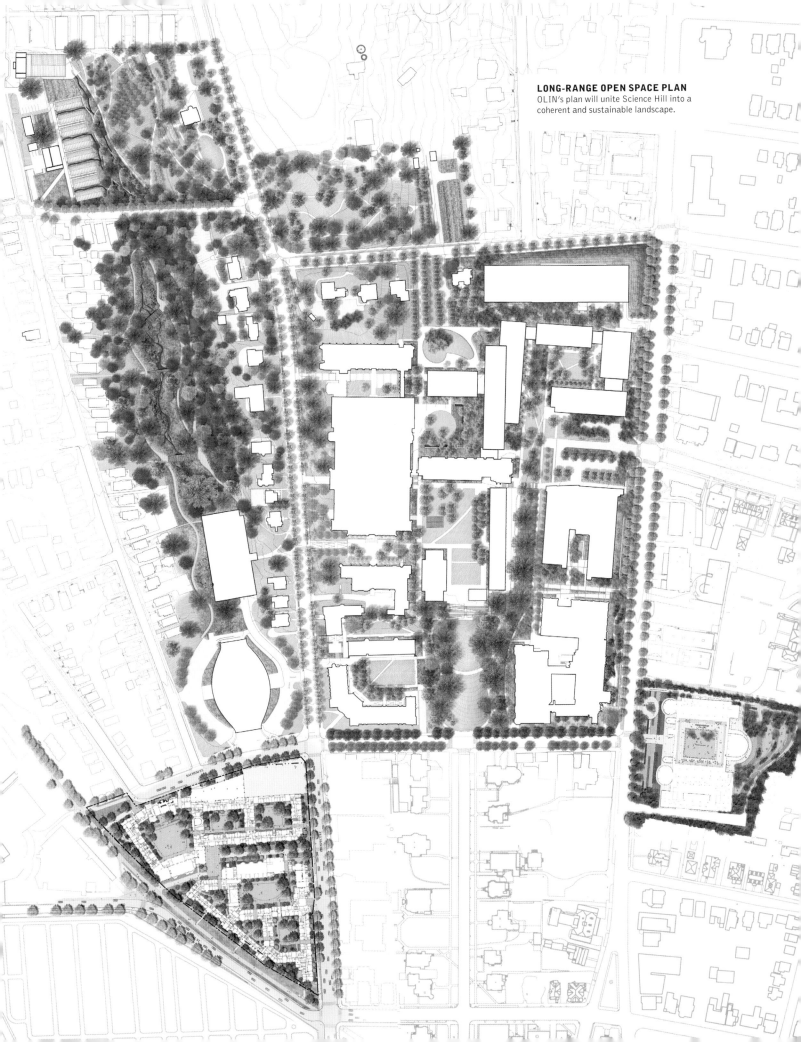

LONG-RANGE OPEN SPACE PLAN
OLIN's plan will unite Science Hill into a coherent and sustainable landscape.

SCIENCE HILL AERIAL The completion of Kroon Hall (foreground) in 2009 created two new, intimate courtyards framed by existing laboratory buildings.

SCIENCE CITY MASTER PLAN SWISS FEDERAL INSTITUTE OF TECHNOLOGY ZURICH

Zürich, Switzerland 2006–13 32 ha (80 acres)
Master planner: KCAP

THE SWISS FEDERAL INSTITUTE OF TECHNOLOGY (ETH) HAS OCCUPIED A KEY POSITION IN THE LIFE OF THE FINANCIAL HUB OF ZÜRICH SINCE ITS FOUNDATION IN 1855.

INFILL CONSTRUCTION The plan proposed an intermixing of new construction and uses: research and teaching buildings, housing, sports facilities, and retail.

Like most traditional European universities, it was initially housed in a grand, single building in the city centre. As it grew, it expanded across the city eventually acquiring a site on the Hönggerberg just outside Zürich. From 1964 to 1976, the Hönggerberg campus was built to house the university's science departments. In common with many satellite science precincts built at this time, it suffered from its isolated location, unwelcoming open spaces, and uninspiring buildings. It was a 9am–5pm commuter campus, overshadowed by fragmentation and remoteness.

In 2005, however, ETH embarked upon an innovative undertaking to transform the single-use compound into a revitalized destination, which it dubbed Science City. Science City would be a vibrant, urbanized centre for cutting-edge teaching and research, drawing scientific talents from around the world to ensure ETH remained competitive at an international level. KCAP Architects produced a master plan to direct this vision.

The plan physically reorganized the campus to transform its layout from a suburban to an urban one. It did not call for razing and rebuilding, but worked within the existing contours of the environment to enhance extant open spaces and identify sites for infill. The design strategy focused heavily on integration and densification. It divided the campus into quarters, and structured each zone upon a basic principle of spatially-interlocking built volumes and open spaces, internal courtyards, and patios. A key principle of the plan was flexibility. For Science City, a fluid framework was requisite in enabling the master plan to adapt to the pace of research and innovation taking place there. In light of this, it prescribed only minimal design principles.

At the heart of the mission of Science City is the furtherance of scientific teaching and research, and to this end several new academic buildings featured within the master plan, the centrepiece being the 2013 Life Sciences Platform. Linked to the pedestrian network running across the site, the new building is an interdisciplinary research centre shaped to foster innovative working practices.

Notwithstanding this scholarly focus, however, one of the most transformative features of the master plan was its residential provision. As part of the goal to create a 24-hour, urban environment, KCAP's plan proposed student accommodation and market housing, interspersed with public open space. Transforming the site from an academic-only precinct into a destination with which the wider public would engage was a high priority. 'We didn't just want to build more labs and buildings, but develop a real campus,' emphasized the project director, Michael Salzmann. 'The goal is to become an intersection between science and society, with its doors open to the public.'[30]

The plan featured new buildings, including conference centre, library, and multifunctional exhibition spaces, that would be open to the public in a bid to encourage interaction and knowledge exchange between the university community and the wider cityscape. 'Publicly accessible zones are located next to highly secure laboratories, offices next to apartment blocks, and conference facilities next to sports centres,' explained master planner Kees Christiaanse. 'This intermixing of different spaces and uses is intended to help turn the existing science hub into a thriving, future-oriented global urban district.'[31]

Many of these planned structures now stand completed. Science City still suffers from the intractability of its satellite location, but the phased implementation of KCAP's plan has undoubtedly breathed new life into the mono-functional precinct while sharing its facilities with a wider territory and community.

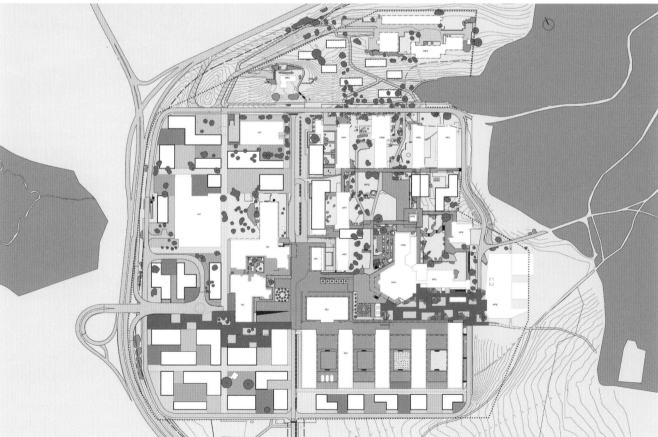

AERIAL CIRCA 2005 The satellite science campus was built in the 1960s and 1970s on the outskirts of Zürich.

MASTER PLAN Within the campus's existing boundary, the plan proposes a dense fabric of large and small buildings, squares, courtyards, and gardens.

SCIENCE CITY VISION The master plan transforms an isolated satellite campus by applying urban principles, identifying opportunities for infill that increase capacity and densify the site.

NOTES

PART 1

1 A. Martin, 'Building a showcase campus, using an I.O.U.', *The New York Times*, 13 December 2012.
2 T. Bowen, 'Recession forces universities to reconsider building plans', *Architectural Record*, February 2009, p. 25.
3 R. Barnett, 'Expanding Universities', *Architectural Record*, November 2012, p. 42.
4 *The Telegraph*, 8 February 2013.
5 Martin, op. cit.
6 *Harvard University Financial Report*, November 2012, p. 5.
7 Similar trends are seen elsewhere. In Australia, May 2012–13 saw a 5.1% rise in university starters. Universities UK, *Patterns and Trends in UK Higher Education*, 2012, pp. 5–7.
8 R. Waite, 'University building boom in battle to win students', *Architects' Journal*, 4 April 2012.
9 E. Gibney, 'A different world', *Times Higher Education*, 31 January 2013, http://www.timeshighereducation.co.uk/features/a-different-world/2001128.article [accessed 18 February 2014].
10 'Eastern stars', *Times Higher Education*, 17 February 2011, http://www.timeshighereducation.co.uk/415193.article [accessed 18 February 2014].
11 Gibney, op.cit.
12 J. Morgan, 'Chinese assets and liabilities for Hong Kong "hub" plans', *Times Higher Education*, 14 February 2013, http://www.timeshighereducation.co.uk/news/chinese-assets-and-liabilities-for-hong-kong-hub-plans/2001484.article [accessed 18 February 2014].
13 *Telegraph*, 19 May 2013.
14 B. Edwards, *Libraries and Learning Resource Centres*, Oxford: Architectural Press, 2001, p. 185.
15 J. Otero-Pailos, 'Restoration redux', *Architectural Record*, February 2012, v. 200, p. 42.
16 S. Kubba, *Handbook of Green Building Design and Construction*, Oxford: Butterworth-Heinemann, 2012, p. 16.
17 S. Roosa and A. Jhaveri, *Carbon Reduction: Policies, Strategies, and Technologies*, Lilburn, GA: Fairmont Press, 2009, p. 104.
18 D. Orenstein, 'Brown builds its future behind familiar façades', *Brown News*, 5 October 2011.
19 A. Oppenheimer Dean, 'School of redesign', *Historic Preservation*, vol. 44, November/December 1992, p. 36.
20 C. Jencks, *The Iconic Building: The Power of Enigma*, London: Francis Lincoln, 2005, p. 7.
21 B. Kamin, 'How stellar are "starchitects"?', *Chicago Tribune*, 27 January 2002.
22 L. Castello, 'The multiple roles of a "starchitecture" museum', *The International Journal of the Inclusive Museum*, vol. 2, no. 1, 2009, p. 46.
23 'Starchitecture on campus', *The Boston Globe*, 22 February 2004.
24 S. Amoroso, 'Icon vs eye-con: the contours of the debate', *Studio*, no. 3, 2012, pp. 20–1.
25 D. Beagle, 'The learning commons in historical context', *Annals of Nagoya University*, v. 7, 2009, p. 35.
26 See for instance www.bradford.ac.uk/student/hub/
27 Multidisciplinary and interdisciplinary research are often used interchangeably but they denote different approaches. A multidisciplinary approach is held to occur when scientists from two or more fields work together on a common subject within the boundaries of their own discipline. An interdisciplinary team crosses the traditional disciplinary boundaries to develop new methods and theories in order to solve problems that transcend single disciplines. One author has created the analogy of a bowl of fruit to describe multidisciplinary research, and a smoothie to portray interdisciplinary studies. In the former each fruit represents a discipline in close proximity to the others, but in the latter the fruit is finely blended so that the distinctive taste of each is no longer recognizable.
A. Repko, *Interdisciplinary Research: Process and Theory*, Thousand Oaks, CA: Sage, 2012, p. 18.
28 M. Harris and K. Holley, 'Constructing the interdisciplinary ivory tower: the planning of interdisciplinary spaces on university campuses', *Planning for Higher Education*, April/June 2008, p. 35; C. Sá, '"Interdisciplinary strategies" in US research universities', *Higher Education: The International Journal of Higher Education and Educational Planning*, vol. 55, no. 5, 2008, p. 19.
29 A. Bretscher, 'Why an interdisciplinary biological research institute now?', *Cornell Chronicle*, 11 December 2008.
30 The US, for example, has seen a steady increase in the funding allotted by the National Science Foundation to multi-investigator projects, as opposed to single-investigator teams. Sá, op. cit., p. 20.

31 P. Goldberger, 'Laboratory conditions', *The New Yorker*, 19 September 2011, p. 88.
32 D. Rhoten, 'Interdisciplinary research: trend or transition', *Items and Issues*, 5, 2004, no. 1–2, pp. 6–9.
33 Organization for Economic Cooperation and Development, 'How is the global talent pool changing?', *Education Indicators in Focus*, May 2012, p. 1.
34 A. Mulder, 'Internet is changing how the world is educated', *The Moscow Times*, 16 January 2013
35 University College London, for example, began operations in Doha's Education City hub using rooms within the Georgetown University building.
36 J. Lane and D. Johnstone (eds), *Universities and Colleges as Economic Drivers*, Albany, NY: SUNY Press, 2012, p. 226.
37 *Chronicle of Higher Education*, 27 February 2012.
38 I. Wylie, 'Campus in the sand', *The Guardian*, 27 May 2008.
39 J. P. C. Roach (ed.), *A History of Cambridgeshire and the Isle of Ely*, vol. 3, London: Oxford University Press, 1938–89, p. 76.
40 D. Perry and W. Wiewel, *The University as Urban Developer: Case Studies and Analysis*, Armonk, NY: M.E. Sharpe, 2005, p. 4.
41 See J. Rodin, *The University & Urban Revival: Out of the Ivory Tower and Into the Streets*, Philadelphia: University of Pennsylvania Press, 2007.
42 Perry and Wiewel, op. cit., pp. 3–4.
43 L. Carroli, 'Kelvin Grove Urban Village: A Strategic Planning Case Study', unpublished report, 2012, p. 7; H. Klaebe, *Sharing Stories: A social history of Kelvin Grove Urban Village*, Bondi Junction, N.S.W.: Focus Publishing, 2006.
44 '£250m Belfast campus will usher in new chapter for city', University of Ulster press release 7 March 2013, http://news.ulster.ac.uk/releases/2013/6868.html [accessed 28 January 2014].
45 'McAslan's masterplan for Lancaster University', *Building Design*, 17 June 2011, pp. 16–17.
46 The Place Activation Plan is a precursor to the Greater Curtin master plan, which maps a wholesale strategic vision for Curtin University's Bentley campus.
47 'McAslan's masterplan for Lancaster University', *Building Design*, 17 June 2011, p. 18.
48 A. Edgecliffe-Johnson and C. Cook, 'Education: From blackboard to keyboard', *Financial Times*, 17 January 2013.
49 'Massive Open Online Courses', Universities UK report, May 2013, p. 2.
50 This discussion is specifically based upon the xMOOC, which is the model provided by the largest platforms.
51 Universities UK, 2013, op cit., p. 7; Edgecliffe-Johnson and Cook, op. cit.
52 Edgecliffe-Johnson and Cook, op. cit.
53 F. Salmon 'Udacity and the Future of Online Universities', 23 January 2012, *Reuters.com*. [Accessed 7 June 2013.]
54 J. Young, 'Will MOOCs change the way professors handle the classroom?', *Chronicle of Higher Education*, 7 November 2013.
55 Edgecliffe-Johnson and Cook, op. cit.
56 C Parr, 'Coursera founder: Mooc credits aren't the real deal', *Times Higher Education*, 28 Jan 2013, http://www.timeshighereducation.co.uk/coursera-founder-mooc-credits-arent-the-real-deal/2001085.article [accessed 18 February 2014]; C. Parr, 'MOOC races: edX goes full throttle, Udacity shifts gears', *Times Higher Education*, 28 November 2013, http://www.timeshighereducation.co.uk/news/moocs-edx-unveils-arab-initiative-udacity-rethinks-lousy-product/2009277.article [accessed 18 February 2014].
57 Universities UK, 2013, op cit., p. 29.
58 'Learning new lessons', *The Economist*, 22 December 2012.
59 Universities UK, 2013, op cit., p. 29.
60 R. Gastil, 'Is there an emerging type of campus design that can both represent and embody an urbanism of opportunity and innovation?', *The Glass House Conversations*, http://glasshouseconversations.org/is-there-an-emerging-type-of-campus-design-that-can-both-represent-and-embody-an-urbanism-of-opportunity-and-innovation-what-are-the-models-to-encourage-emulate-and-question/ [accessed 6 February 2014].
61 Lane and Johnstone, op. cit., p. 226.
62 'How to talk about liberal education (if you must)', *The Boston Globe*, 21 November 2004; 'Partnering with industry', *Guardian*, 31 July 2012.
63 J. Morgan, 'Technology and innovation at the core of the Big Apple', *Times Higher Education*, 12 January 2012, http://www.timeshighereducation.co.uk/news/technology-and-innovation-at-the-core-of-the-big-apple/418687.article, [accessed 18 February 2014].

PART 2

1 Central Saint Martins was formed following the merger of the Central School of Art and Design (founded 1896) and Saint Martins School of Art (founded 1854).
2 The Granary Building was Grade II Listed in 1978.
3 J. Glancey, 'Central Saint Martins: Inside the art factory', *The Guardian*, 13 December 2011.
4 The roof of the eastern transit shed was rebuilt to illuminate the studios but followed its original profile.
5 R. Wentworth, 'Central St Martins, King's Cross, London, by Stanton Williams', *Building Design*, 21 October 2011, p. 23.
6 P. Clemence, 'The East Lansing effect', *The Metropolis Blog*, http://www.metropolismag.com/pov/20121126/the-east-lansing-effect#more-27577 [accessed 25 June 2013].
7 D. D'Arcy, 'Zaha Hadid-designed Broad Museum "redirects perceptions"', *The National*, 13 November 2013.
8 'MSU's shining jewel revealed', *Lansing State Journal*, 11 November 2012.
9 B. Broome, 'Eli and Edythe Broad Art Museum', *Architectural Record*, January 2013, p. 92.
10 'The Eli and Edythe Broad Art Museum; Architects: Zaha Hadid Architects', *Icon*, no. 117, March 2013, pp. 60–1.
11 Broome, ibid. p. 94.
12 S. Cox, 'The Eli and Edythe Broad Art Museum', *The Architect's Newspaper*, 15 November 2012.
13 G. Greer, 'Frank Gehry's new building looks like five scrunched-up brown bags', *The Guardian*, 9 January 2011.
14 In 2006, its landmark tower building was voted the ugliest structure in Sydney. 'Ugly talk strikes a chord in city's heart', *The Sydney Morning Herald*, 1 November 2006.
15 E. Farrelly, 'Gehry has designed a building that is more about him than us', *The Age*, 13 January 2011.
16 Greer, ibid.
17 'Lend Lease lands bid to build Gehry-designed "paper bag" project', *The Sydney Morning Herald*, 23 November 2012.
18 'Wilkinson Eyre's Exeter Forum', *Architecture Today*, June 2012, p. 34.
19 'Wilkinson Eyre's Exeter Forum', *Architecture Today*, June 2012, p. 40–2.
20 'Wilkinson Eyre's Exeter Forum', *Architecture Today*, June 2012, p. 42.
21 59 per cent of those questioned said they spend between one and five more hours on campus each day since Hub Central opened. This compares to statistics that formed the original business case for the new space, which revealed that before its opening 87 per cent of students and staff moved off campus just to eat lunch.
22 'Studying on the staircase', *Werk, Bauen and Wohnen*, September 2013, p. 49.
23 K. Rosenfield, 'Cornell releases preliminary renderings of NYC Tech Campus', *Architectural Record*, 15 October 2012.
24 'China's polite society', *Times Higher Education*, 6 June 2013, http://www.timeshighereducation.co.uk/comment/opinion/chinas-polite-society/2004325.article [accessed 6 February 2013].
25 'Cambridge 2.0 – the £1 billion University development that you should probably know more about', *TCS*, 15 October 2012.
26 Ibid.
27 C. Cookson, 'Building on London's scientific tradition', *Financial Times*, 4 December 2013.
28 The third campus zone, East Campus, is addressed but slightly in Sasaki's study. This 21-hectare (52-acre) site is much less densely developed than the other two zones and with minimal connections to them.
29 The economic crisis caused Yale to scale down and postpone some of its intended new buildings, such as the Kline Chemistry Laboratory which is now being renovated rather than rebuilt.
30 Y. Hager, 'A town called science,' *Chemistry World*, February 2008, http://www.rsc.org/chemistryworld/Issues/2008/February/ATownCalledScience.asp [accessed 25 June 2013].
31 K. Hoeger and K. Christiaanse, *Campus and the City*, Zurich: GTA Verlag, 2007, pp. 236–7.